Developing]

MAKING ORGANIZATIONS MORE HUMAN ————————

Followership

Catalyzing your leadership practice

Publisher's note

Every effort has been made to ensure information contained in this publication is accurate at the time of going to press. Neither the publishers nor any of the contributors can accept responsibility for any errors or omissions, however caused, nor for any loss or damage occasioned to any person acting, or refraining from action, as a result of the material in this publication.

Users and readers of this publication may copy portions of the material for personal use, internal reports, or reports to clients provided that such articles (or portions of articles) are attributed to this publication by name, the individual contributor of the portion uses and publisher.

IEDP Ideas for Leaders Ltd
42 Moray Place, Edinburgh, EH3 6BT
www.ideasforleaders.com

in association with the Center for the Future of Organization at the Drucker School of Management
www.futureorg.org

Publishers: Roland Deiser and Roddy Millar
Editor-in-Chief: Roddy Millar
Senior Editor: Roland Deiser
Associate Editors: Saar Ben-Attar (Africa), Suzie Lewis (Europe) Conrado Schlochauer (LatAm), Ravi Shankar (SE Asia)
Art Direction: Nick Mortimer – nickmortimer.co.uk

Copyright ©2024 IEDP Ideas for Leaders Ltd and contributors

ISBN 978-1-91-552926-8 (Paperback)
ISBN 978-1-91-552927-5 (e-Pub)
ISSN 2044-2203 (Developing Leaders Quarterly)

www.developingleadersquarterly.com

Contents

The title of this publication is *Developing Leaders Quarterly*, and the name of our business that publishes it is *Ideas for Leaders*. Our focus has always been on leadership and the impact it makes on organizations. And we are not unusual in that.

Search Amazon for Leadership books and you get over 60,000 results, which is pretty much the tip of the iceberg. Famously, ask for a definition of leadership and you will get a not dissimilar number of answers too; but one thing we can probably all agree on is that if no-one follows you, then you are not leading anyone.

Followers have tended to be overlooked in the multitude of discussions around leadership, and yet they are not just critical to leadership, they are what makes leaders. As the title of the book by **Marc and Sam Hurwitz** who write the opening articles in this issue states 'Leadership is half the story'. Followers are the other side of the same coin. And that metaphor is important, as – just like leadership – followership does not stand on its own either. They can only be understood in terms of their connection to one another. That goes as much for leadership as it does for followership.

So, I am thrilled we have this issue to highlight the importance of followership in the exploration of what we normally term 'leadership development'.

It is vital to understand that Followership is very different from just 'following'. Following is a passive role, whereas followership is very definitely an active one. It requires awareness, curiosity, initiative, and - to harness the title of the book of our third article's author, **Ira Chaleff** – courage.

These capacities are exciting, engaging and motivating ones to have and put into practice – so leaders who can enable the conditions for good followership will be developing a much more engaged and hopefully productive organization.

The challenge for the fast-growing number of promoters of Followership is primarily a semantic one. We have grown-up seeing 'being a leader' as the mark of success, and typically it is leaders who are best remunerated – so who wants to be a 'follower' in such circumstances. The reality is that we are all followers – even leaders are followers. The CEO has to follow the Board, and the Board the shareholders; presidents and prime ministers follow their electorate by-and-large.

We all need to understand how followership works, what impact it has on organizations, and how it interacts with the tenets of leadership. Just as we need to understand how leaders can only work within the parameters their followers permit them. The conundrum is that leaders are in thrall to their followers, but followers' greatest power is when they are united, which usually means having a leader.

I hope that the selection of pieces we have curated here from some of the leading thinkers on followership will stimulate you and make you more interested in the topic. As well as the two pieces above, I am delighted to have **Langley Sharp** providing a view drawing on the UK's Centre of Army Leadership doctrine on Followership; **Basil Read III** sharing his experiences with two large organizations that have embraced followership in the US; **Julie Newman** on her involvement with bringing followership to a non-profit; and **Christian Monö**'s wonderful piece highlighting that we use followership naturally in many contexts, so why not at work?

As ever we dilute the focus with other pieces all designed to spark and engage your leadership thinking. Executive coach **Mark McCartney**, who has been taking a sabbatical in South America with his family, posits some questions we should ponder on the benefits of pausing and reflecting. **Wendy Shepherd** of Cranfield School of Management writes on how directly seeking ROI for leadership programs is really not a Holy Grail. And there is a piece on things we can learn from the Maasai – where at least the photos are good!

As always, we are keen to hear your thoughts, comments and suggestions on these and future topics – please email us with them.

Roddy   Roland

Roddy Millar, Editorial Director and Co-publisher
Roland Deiser, Co-publisher

Thinking imprinted.

The first step on any leadership development process is to create space and condition for reflection on your leadership practice.

Multiple studies have concluded that we absorb and digest information better when we read off the printed page. Reading is focused, uninterrupted and, with the chance to note down our own thoughts in the margins, print allows us to actively engage with the subject.

To embed the change, Developing Leaders Quarterly is best in print.

Developing Leaders Quarterly print edition is ideally formatted to slip into your pocket, bag or briefcase to read when you find you have a few minutes to spare before a business guest arrives, while commuting, at the airport...

By Marc and Samantha Hurwitz

Followership Matters

Everyone is a follower

n Canada, we have a quick service restaurant named Tim Hortons that is a national obsession. From its double-double (double cream, double sugar, in a unique proprietary blend of coffee) to its hot weather equivalent, the Iced Capp, to its TimBits which come in two forms: a party pack box of 12, 24 or 48 multi-flavoured sugary donut holes and a hockey league for 4 to 8 year olds, equally sweet and delightful.

Tim Horton's is so iconic and integral to Canadian culture that the Canadian Armed Forces had a pop-up Tim Horton's in Kandahar, Afghanistan during the war. Recently, our daughter and son travelled to Singapore, Thailand and Dubai, and were delighted to discover their beloved Timmys in all three locations. We just visited Glasgow for the first time and saw one right across

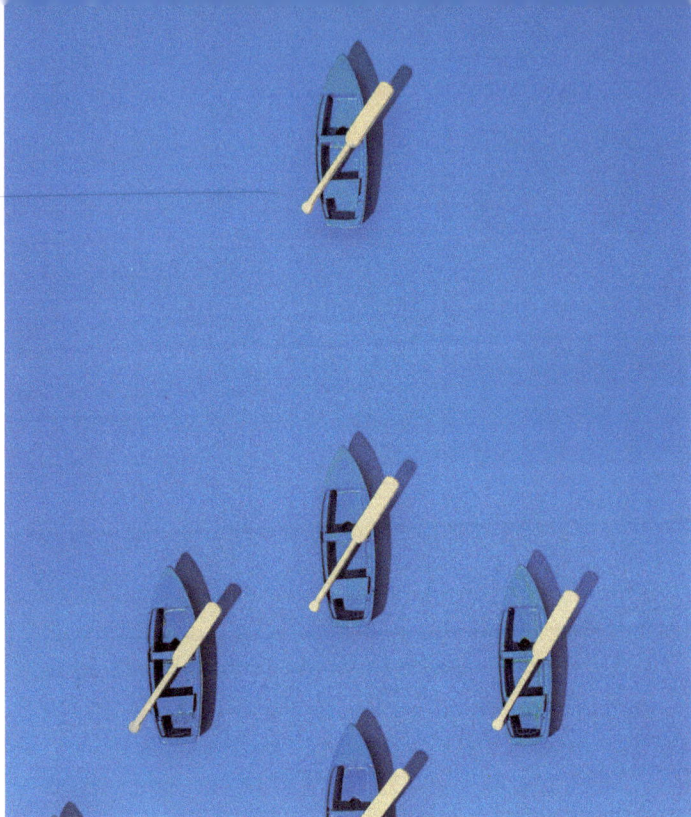

from Strathclyde University, the host of the 2024 Global Followership Conference.

We had the pleasure of working with one of Tim Horton's most successful franchisees, the Seth family. At the time, they owned over 50 locations and garnered 2x to 3x higher profitability than average stores. They were the crown jewel of the franchise.

The secret to their success, according to their CEO,

Their current style of followership could be transformed from a passive, compliance-oriented approach to an active, proactive, initiative-taking style.

Amit, was believing deeply in the potential of each team member and continually investing in their learning and development. When we met him, he had trained all his senior leadership team, store managers and assistant store managers on Servant Leadership. The year after, he brought us in to teach everyone Followership. Specifically, Amit envisioned his organization could reach higher performance if their current style of followership could be transformed from a passive, compliance-oriented approach to an active, proactive, initiative-taking style, the kind we talk about in our book, *Leadership is Half the Story*.

One day, we were sitting in one of his restaurants, chatting with the store manager and looking out the window waiting for Amit to arrive for a meeting. We saw him drive into the parking lot in his BMW 8-series, get out of the car, and look around. Clearly, he saw something that did not please him at all. Amit, in his immaculate business suit, started picking up litter in the parking lot. When he had a handful, he came over to the store, put it in the trash, and went back out. The store manager followed him out and they both continued cleaning.

We have mused on this small incident – this leadership-followership moment – for years, now. It perfectly illustrates how leading and following can work, and we have thought on how it might work even better.

Imagine, for a moment, that you were the store manager in this situation. Most of the time, within the store, you lead. However, when Amit is around, you step into the role of follower. This is a similar position that most leaders find themselves in: sometimes you lead and sometimes you follow, whether you are a frontline manager or even the CEO, following their Board of Directors.

Back to the scenario: imagine you notice your boss picking up the trash in the parking lot. What are all the things you might do? What would your likely response be?

We can imagine four possibilities:

1. You do what the store manager actually did in this case, you go out and help by doing the same thing. You *mimic* the leader. This might be described as an example of good followership.

2. Perhaps, though, you spot an opportunity for greater efficiency and safety. You bring a couple of pairs of rubber gloves and empty rubbish bags with you, speed-

ing up the process, helping the boss stay clean and keeping the rubbish outside the restaurant. You *complement* what the leader does. This is strong followership.

3. How might you go even further? You could do all the above and engage other team members in various ways. For example, you could set up a cleaning schedule for the parking lot so that there will never be a time in the future where the boss shows up and the lot is messy. Or you could bring the topic to the next team meeting and ask team members for all their suggestions for ensuring this never happens again. In other words, you *take initiative* that fulfills the goals of the boss, even without them having to ask you for it. This is an expert level of followership.

4. Of course, there is a fourth option. You could stay in the restaurant, thinking how great it is that your boss is cleaning the parking lot. In fact, the next time the lot needs cleaning, you will invite him over again. That is poor followership because you missed the point.

We have found this response typology – mimicry, complementarity, and initiative-taking – to be a useful way to think about the following role and the positive impact it can create in partnership with the person leading.

Leadership theories generally suggest that there is

With the rise of Thomas Carlyle's Great Man Theory of Leadership the importance of following and followership was forgotten.

only one possible response: if you do A in your leadership role, people will inevitably respond with B. We see our job as picking up after this sort of leadership rubbish because it is not true. In the Tim Horton's scenario above, the success of Amit's leadership style depended on how his team responded to it. If his team followed in the right ways, he was successful. That was why he brought us in, because Servant Leadership – taking on a follower role even when you are the formal leader – only works if the people in formal follower roles are willing to lead, and know how and when to do so. There is no point serving if no-one else takes the lead. There is no point "leading the way" if team members are unwilling, unclear or unable to mimic the person leading. In a partnership, both partners need to understand and enact their roles well while also being aware of what the other is doing so they can create a suitable response.

Why Followership?

Thoughtful followership is just as important to outcomes as thoughtful leadership. In a meta-analysis on the value of strong followership on success, organizations with one standard deviation better followership showed an improvement of 17-43% on virtually every significant metric: productivity, quality, service levels, customer satisfaction, engagement scores, top-line results, and even bottom-line profits. Followership matters, yet few HR and Organization Development professionals know about it, few leaders mentor it explicitly with their teams, and even fewer organizations provide training on it. This is a gap; significant organizational value is being left on the table.

Interestingly, ideas of what constitute great followership are as old as ideas about great leadership. The earliest recorded story, The Epic of Gilgamesh, is as much about Gilgamesh learning to lead as it is about Enkidu - his slave and later friend - following courageously and well.

One thread remained constant: it was all about what the leader did, as if the response by followers was predictable, controllable, and automatic. How people respond to what you do is as important as what you do.

How Did We Get Here: A Brief Look at Leadership Research

It was not until the 19th Century, with the rise of Thomas Carlyle's Great Man Theory of Leadership, that the importance of following and followership was forgotten. Why is that? What happened to make us forget half the story? The answer lies in the rise of industrialization.

With manufacturing came standardization, where people became akin to the parts of a clock, ticking along doing the same tasks over-and-over again. The desire to get all the right parts working in exactly the right way led to the creation of an approach during the latter part of the 19th Century known as Scientific Management or Taylorism. The prime architect of this approach - Frederick Taylor - noted that the job of a leader was about *"knowing exactly what you want men to do, and then seeing that they do it in the best and cheapest way."* He formalized and provided guidance on the best ways to organize, the best ways to standardize, and the best ways to work by developing and applying ideas such as time-and-motion studies. Henry Ford advanced Taylor's ideas to create the modern assembly line in the early twentieth century. In this highly leader-centric view of the world, the most important leadership problem was about figuring out who can arrange and train all the parts to perform best. And what better way to answer this than to study the traits of successful leaders.

Almost the entirety of the first half of the 20th century was spent searching and research-

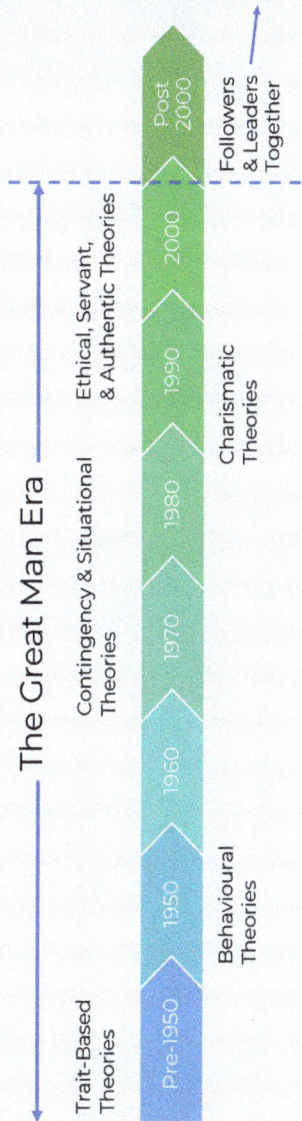

Figure 1: History of Leadership Theories

An eliciting behaviour might be telling your leader you need more positive feedback - what you are doing is trying to get them to be more transformational in their approach

ing the traits of "Great Men." Hundreds of possibilities were suggested and evidence was provided for the relative importance of each trait, some as prosaic as the height of an individual, some ridiculous such as the length of an individual's index finger, and some that seemed quite reasonable such as cognitive ability. Finally, in 1948, R.M. Stodgill published a seminal paper that showed statistically there were no traits correlated more with leaders than followers. For the next 40 years, from about 1950-1990 (see Figure 1), a variety of other theories were proposed. First came Task Approach vs. People

Focus and other behavioural ideas of what defines great leadership, then came the rise of charismatic theories such as Transformational Leadership as well as a broad array of others including Servant Leadership, Authentic Leadership, Leader-Member Exchange, Ethical Leadership, and more. But one thread remained constant: it was all about what the leader did, as if the response by followers was predictable, controllable, and automatic. Anyone who has worked in the day-to-day world of a frontline or middle manager knows this just isn't so. How people respond to what you do is as important as what you do.

Followership Research

We interviewed 40 senior managers about what they have learned about followership over their long careers. The results were intriguing. Qualitative analysis of the data showed that their success depended on two dimensions (see Figure 2). The first dimension is what we call **Reflexive Followership:** the ability to reflect on what the leader is trying to do and figure out how to enhance it. For example, if a leader is attempting to be transformational by providing encouragement, it is equally important to "be" encouraged. In other words, actively support the leader's skills and behaviours in order to further their goals. Think about an interaction you have had with your team members, for example. When you asked them to

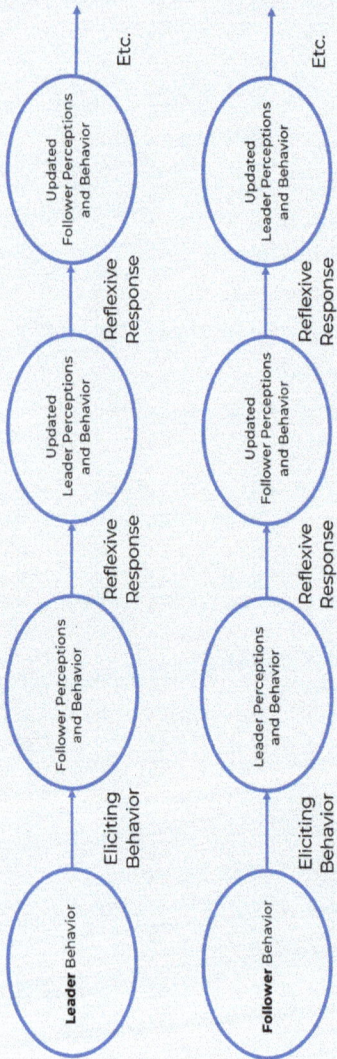

Figure 2: Reflexive & Eliciting Dimensions

follow your lead (mimicry), did they? And when there were different possible responses, such as in the Tim Horton's case, did they figure out which was the best option and do that? Do your followers regularly ask you if they applied the best response in a situation? And do you trust that they deeply understand the goals you are trying to achieve before they set out and take action?

The second dimension of excellent followership is what we call **Eliciting Leadership**. These are behaviours initi-

75% of senior women's careers are derailed because of poor followership, more than for any other reason.

ated by the follower that shape their leader's behaviour to make the partnership more effective. For example, an eliciting behaviour might be telling your leader you need more positive feedback - what you are doing is trying to get them to be more transformational in their approach. It is more than a response to what the leader does, it actively builds a stronger partnership from the bottom up.

By the way, the other piece of sage advice the senior managers gave was that their career success depended on their skills as a follower at least as much if not more than their skills as a leader. Think about it: What does your leader observe more of, your leadership skills or your followership skills? Research supports the conclusion that getting promoted depends on your followership skills. What's more, the higher in an organization you rise, the more important those followership skills are to your success (see Figure 3). Being a poor follower as a front-line staff may not end your career, but being a poor follower in the C-suite will, as is evidenced by the number of CEOs, even high-profile ones, who experience a precipitous fall from grace. In a literature survey we did on executive derailment – either being fired or

The agility to show up as a strong leader when needed and then to pivot to strong follower when someone else is leading is truly the mark of excellence. It is what distinguishes someone who is in service to the mission of the organization rather than to themselves.

career-stalling – one of the top three reasons in every article was followership. One PhD thesis on female executives, for example, found that 75% of senior women's careers derailed because of poor followership, more than for any other reason.

We have spent the last 20 years researching, reading, writing, creating courses, and training people on leadership and followership. The feedback we get time and again is that once people learn about followership, it is the key that unlocks everything else. If leadership is like seeing with one eye closed, followership and leadership are like seeing with two eyes; everything becomes clearer and more three-dimensional.

Who is a Follower?

One of the mistaken beliefs front-line employees ascribe to is that the minute they are promoted to team lead, they are now a leader not a follower. The reality is quite different for three reasons. First of all, pretty much everyone follows someone else. A team lead follows their manager (or director), the VP follows the CEO, the CEO follows the Board of Directors or Governors, and the Governors follow their stakeholders. One of the dysfunctions we have noted in senior managers happens when they stop seeing themselves as a follower and only focus on their leader role. We had a chat a few years back with the #1 rated executive coach in the world, Marshall Goldsmith. His clients are almost all C-suite executives of major corporations. Samantha asked him this simple question: "How many of your coaching assignments are about fixing poor followership rather than poor leadership?" He took

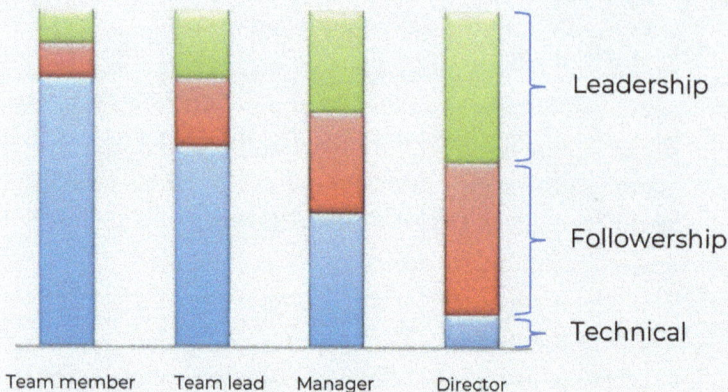

Figure 3: Followership Importance by Level

a few moments to think about it, because no-one had asked him about followership before, and then replied, "Half." The next 15 minutes were Goldsmith telling funny and sometimes salty stories (he is quite the story-teller) about some of his most memorable followership coaching clients.

The second reason is deeper and more important: leadership is not about where you are located in an organizational chart, leadership is about the act of leading. An organizational chart indicates who has formal authority and power, not who is leading. In any high functioning team, sometimes you lead and sometimes you

Following is not just about who you follow but also what you follow.

follow. It does not matter who is the boss or manager or formal leader. The more collaborative the team, the more often leading and following roles switch between people from task to task. You might lead a meeting, a project, or process, and your team members might end up leading you at another time. The agility to show up as a strong leader when needed and then to pivot to strong follower when someone else is leading is truly the mark of excellence. It is what distinguishes someone who is in service to the mission of the organization rather than to themselves.

And this leads us to the third and most important point: following is not just about who you follow but also what you follow. Think about all the ideas, structures, and frameworks you follow in a given day. That list might include following your professional ethics if you are an engineer or accountant, or your values, or the team objectives, or the mission of the organization. Dynamically supporting the mission of your team or organization by supporting your leader is how you serve the wider good. Focusing only on supporting your boss or, worse yet, your own career is what gives followership a bad name.

Main Followership Ideas

Analysis of three sources – interviews, survey, literature review – found widespread consensus on these key ideas:

1. **Everyone is a leader and a follower**, from frontline employees to the CEO.
2. **Followership is vital to both individual and organizational success**.
3. Leadership and followership are much more than a place in a hierarchy. **Leadership and followership are the essential dynamic system that helps teams and organizations thrive.**
4. **Leadership and followership are active roles**. If you embrace both roles, become expert at both, and learn to mentor both, then every team and organization you are part of will be better.

In the rest of this journal issue, you will read a lot more about followership, different views of it, what can be accomplished with it, and why it matters. Just as there is no one way to lead, there are multiple perspectives on followership. However, we would like to leave you with a few best practices:

1. Keep your leader well informed in an efficient and timely manner.
2. Stimulate the right leadership actions through your communications.
3. Provide useful and timely decision support.
4. Work hard to support changes your leader is making. Be a decision advocate rather than a devil's advocate.
5. Provide good rationale for your opinions, ideas and recommendations.
6. Be accountable for your own engagement; it is not someone else's job to engage you or inspire you.
7. Work hard to build a relationship with your leader.

Marc Hurwitz is Chief Insight Officer for FliP University, a training company, and is an Associate Director in the Conrad School of Entrepreneurship and Business at University of Waterloo. He has a doctorate in cognitive neuroscience and consults on 21st century leadership, followership, and collaborations.

Samantha Hurwitz is a leadership and followership coach, trainer and consultant with many years of corporate experience. With Marc she is co-founder of FliP University (Followership, Leadership, innovation and Partnership)

They are co-authors of Leadership is Half the Story: A fresh look at followership, leadership and collaboration.

By Christian Monö

Natural Followership and Why it is Important

Since the early 1900s, the idea of leadership has infiltrated every facet of society. It is sought after, trained for, discussed, and analyzed everywhere – from business and politics to sports and arts. But what *is* a leader? What is the official definition? If you don't know, it is because there isn't one. Scholars and experts cannot agree on what a leader is. The only thing they agree upon is that leaders are important. Yet, how do we know leaders are important if we don't know what a leader is?

Most theories on leadership and followership have been crafted by people who view the world from a leader perspective – followers are generally regarded as "the collective" who react rather than influence their surroundings.

Despite this uncertainty, organizations around the world invest billions of dollars in leadership development every year. In contrast, investments in followership are almost non-existent. This is largely due to our perception of followers. People still see followers as passive, uncritical minions, but I have spent almost two decades exploring what I term *natural followership*. That is, I have studied *why* and *how* people follow leaders when free of hierarchies and dominance. As you read on, you will see that true followership is far more fascinating than commonly believed.

Why having a followership perspective can change our view of the world

My interest in followership began in early 2007 after a conversation with a relative. He had been pondering why companies were investing time and money in leadership

and not followership. His question intrigued me and for the next few weeks I spent hours searching for relevant books, articles, and research papers on the topic. There was not much out there at the time and what I found was mostly irrelevant. I wanted to know *why* people follow each other, but scholars, even those writing about followership, were generally more interested in how followers should be led.

Frustrated, I gave up and decided to start anew. I remember writing on a piece of paper, "What makes me want to follow someone else?" Little did I know that at that moment, I chose a *follower perspective*, and it would transform my life.

Most theories on leadership and followership have been crafted by people who view the world from a *leader perspective* – that is, they view the world from a leader's lens. With this perspective, followers are generally regarded as "the collective" who *react* rather than *influence* their surroundings. Leaders, on the other hand, are expected to influence their surroundings, which is why companies invest in leadership and not followership.

I find this perspective peculiar. If leaders are expected to influence their followers, then what is the point of living in a democracy? The term "democracy" comes from the Greek *demos*, meaning "people", and *kratos* meaning "rule". In other words, democracy means rule by the people. But how can we believe in democracy and at the same time argue that people must be led?

The problem is that we are caught in a loop where our focus on leadership only amplifies our attention on it. This has led to *inattentional blindness* so that we only see leadership as the solution to all our problems. As a result, the leadership industry revolves around two key questions - "*what* makes someone a leader?" and "how does one *become* a leader?"

These two questions assume there are specific factors that turn people into followers, and so experts and scholars have spent decades chasing what I call the *Holy Grail of Leadership*. By this, I mean they are trying

The leadership industry revolves around two key questions - "what makes someone a leader?" and "how does one become a leader?"

to identify a *recipe* on how one can become a leader. I am sure you have seen articles with titles such as "10 Steps to Becoming a Great Leader" or "7 Steps to Becoming an Effective Leader".

With a follower perspective it seems unlikely that there is a formula on how to become a leader. Followers are *human beings* not passive robots waiting to be switched on. We all have different thoughts, opinions, and feelings. If we cannot agree on what political party to vote for or which movie is worth watching, why would we all want to follow the same person?

It is time we re-evaluate our focus on leadership, and a good place to start is by letting go of the idea of the Holy Grail of Leadership. Instead of focusing on what makes someone a leader and how to become one, we could explore the question "*who* determines if someone is a leader?". This is a far more interesting question. It allows for the possibility that people *choose* their followership.

To understand true followership, we must explore the subject in a more natural environment, and that means turning to our history.

In search of natural leadership and followership

If you were a zoologist studying the natural behaviour of lions, would you conduct your research in a zoo or in the wild?

For years, I have asked workshop participants this question and so far, not a single person has answered "the zoo". Clearly, it makes sense that to identify an animal's innate behaviour, one must study them in their natural environment. Yet, when it comes to research on leadership and followership, the vast majority has been conducted in *unnatural* environments, most typically workplaces.

In many ways, the workplace is the human equivalent of a zoo. Employment is based on a *contract* between employer and employee. This contract includes everything from job description to wages and benefits. In most organizations, you will also be given a manager whose orders you are expected to follow, regardless of your feelings for this person.

In other words, much like animals in a zoo, an employee's behaviour is directed and controlled by external factors that affect people's behaviour. If we try to examine leadership and followership in such environments, we run the risk of making flawed assumptions, like confusing leadership with with hierarchical authority. So, to understand true followership, we must explore the subject in a more natural environment, and that means turning to our history.

Homo sapiens made their debut in Africa approximately 300,000 years ago. As far as we know, our ancestors spent the first 240,000 years of their existence in small, so-called 'band societies'. These were groups of no more than 20-40 individuals living as nomadic hunter and gatherers.

Individual freedom was greatly valued, while there was a clear aversion to hierarchical behaviour, especially dominance. To protect equality and freedom, our ancestors appear to have invested significant effort in preventing individuals from gaining power and status.

Thanks to interdisciplinary cooperation, we have a fairly good idea of how band societies traditionally lived and behaved. Not being hierarchically structured, they lacked formal decision-makers, institutions, laws, and contracts. Individual freedom was greatly valued, while there was a clear aversion to hierarchical behaviour, especially dominance.[1] To protect equality and freedom, our ancestors appear to have invested significant effort in preventing individuals from gaining power and status.[2] For instance, if someone displayed a desire to dominate others, the group intervened.[3] Anthropologist Christo-

---

1   Boehm, C. (Juni 1993) Egalitarian Behavior and Reverse Dominance Hierarchy. Current Anthropology 34, no. 3. p 227

2   Woodburn J. (September 1982) Egalitarian Societies. Man. New Series. Vol.17. No3. p. 433

3   Wiessner, P. (April 2002) The Vines of Complexity: Egalitarian Structures and the Institutionalization of Inequality Among the Enga. Current Anthropology Vol. 43, no. 2. p 235

pher Boehm referred to this behaviour as *Reverse Dominance Hierarchy*.[4] Rather than one person monitoring and controlling the group, it was the other way around. The group collectively protected individual freedom. Anyone displaying qualities like selfishness, bossiness, or a desire to appear superior, were met with criticism and scorn.[5]

Does this mean band societies lacked leaders? Not necessarily, but to identify their leaders, we must reconsider our definition of what a leader is.

Leader rotation and collaborationship

When people discuss leaders today, they often picture individuals with a particular level of influence and a status *that remains relatively constant over time*. Managers are leaders during work hours, and a president is a leader while holding that position. But in band societies, where there were no formal decision-makers, people had a far more ingenious strategy. They would follow *different individuals depending on their vision, needs or objectives*.

For instance, when hunting, members tended to follow the hunter that was most skilled or successful,

4   Boehm, C. (Juni 1993) Egalitarian Behavior and Reverse Dominance Hierarchy. Current Anthropology 34, no. 3. p 236

5   Boehm, C. (Juni 1999) Hierarchy in the Forest: The Evolution of Egalitarian Behavior. Cambridge, MA, USA: Harvard University Press. pp 73-74

When socializing with friends, we do not identify a decision-maker; instead, we make use of each other's differences. Whatever challenge we are facing, we will turn to the person best suited to help us.

but when facing other challenges, like needing to solve a conflict or delivering a baby, people would follow someone else. This does not mean that skilled individuals could claim the role as leader, or even assume they would be asked to lead the others. Anyone who displayed signs of dominance was ridiculed and ignored. Instead, the members chose their leaders based on what they thought was best for the group at any given time.

In other words, true leaders are more like *guides* than decision-makers. They are used as tools to help a group reach a common goal, objective, or vision.

This form of *leader rotation*, as I call it, has been observed in egalitarian band societies worldwide. It is so prominent in these societies that even when members face similar tasks, leadership will rotate between different individuals.[6] I would even go so far as to argue that

---

6   Silberbauer, G. "Political Process in G/wi Bands." in Politics and History in Band Societies. Cambridge University Press, p 29.

leader rotation is one of the oldest and most fundamental features of human interaction. Even today, people engage in leader rotation without realizing it. When socializing with friends, we do not identify a decision-maker; instead, we make use of each other's differences. We know who among our friends is the best organizer, the most adventurous, creative, a better listener, etc. Whatever challenge we are facing, we will turn to the person best suited to help us.

This is important to understand. It would be ineffective and frankly absurd for a group to follow a single individual *all the time*. It would make the group weak, not strong.

To conclude, true leadership and followership arise when people join forces to build synergies, thus maximizing the chances of reaching a common goal or vision. I have chosen to call this process *collaborationship*, and without it, there is no reason for people to lead and follow one another.

Two different relationships

Once we have identified the process of natural followership, we can conclude that there are two central relationships which are often confused. One is the relationship between leader and follower. The second is between decision-maker and subordinate.

The relationship between leader and follower is deeply rooted in human nature, while the relationship between decision-maker and subordinate is socially constructed. Understanding the difference between these two relationships is crucial if we want to bring about change in our organizations and societies.

The relationship between decision-makers and subordinates is built on power dynamics where the decision-maker holds power over the subordinates. Between leaders and followers, it is the latter who wield power over the leader. People always choose their leaders, just as they choose when they want to follow and for how long. Thus, we can define ourselves as **followers** *when we voluntarily choose to follow someone else's directives for a limited period of time to achieve a purpose shared with the leader and other followers.* This means that we are **leaders** *when someone temporarily gives us the task to guide them toward a shared goal or vision.*

The relationship between decision-makers and subordinates, such as the one between a manager and employees, is different. **Decision-makers** possess the right or power to make decisions for a group of people, granting them a formal role that others must adhere to, whether they want to or not.

Subordinates, on the other hand, are someone under the authority or control of another and are often regarded as less important than his or her superiors.

While the relationship between leaders and followers revolves around a shared purpose, the relationship between decision-makers and subordinates is typically rooted in tasks or areas of responsibility. That means the relationship between decision-makers and subordinates can persist even if the parties are driven by entirely different visions and goals. For example, you can be employed at a company, fulfil your job duties, comply with your boss, and still be entirely disinterested in the company's vision.

'll hopefully grow
ocused on who is
ng and following,
more focused on
ow to build great
ollaborationship.

We are standing at a crossroad – now what?

In 1992, American management professor Robert E. Kelley published *The Power of Followership*. To my knowledge, it was the first English-speaking book focusing solely on followership. Three years later, the now renowned followership expert, Ira Chaleff, published his book, *The Courageous Follower*.

When I started my work on followership in 2007, Kelley's book was already out of print. Interestingly, Chaleff's book remains one of the most popular books on followership today. Why is it that two books that were published at roughly the same time, discuss the importance of followers, are well-written, and have the word followership in the title met such different fates?

Well, while both books spotlighted followership, Kelley's book *confronted* the leadership industry. He had an entire chapter titled: "Warning: Leadership May Be Hazardous for You." He claimed leaders contribute no more than 20 percent to the success of most organizations and coined the term "Leadership Myth" to describe people's irrational belief in leaders and their significance.

Chaleff, on the other hand, chose a different and perhaps wiser approach. Instead of challenging the leadership industry, he presented followers in a manner that fitted the traditional perspectives on leadership. In his book he describes followers as subordinates whose primary focus is to *serve* and *support* their leaders. With this careful approach, Chaleff cleverly avoided a confrontation with the leadership industry.

While I admire Kelley for daring to challenge the industry at a time when the global interest in leadership was at its peak, we probably have Chaleff to thank for today's growing interest in followership. It is easier for people to accept followership as a concept when it does not challenge their existing perspectives.

Followership is gaining worldwide attention, and we are standing at a crossroad. If we continue to adapt followership so it fits the leadership industry's preconceived view of the world, then we won't learn anything new. We will have the same leadership theories, only packaged differently.

If, on the other hand, we are genuinely interested in what makes people follow one another, then we must have the courage to view the world from the followers' perspective. If we do this with an open mind, followership will lead us to new discoveries. With time, we will hopefully grow less focused on who is leading and following, and more focused on how to build great collaborationship.

Of course, changing perspective is not easy. As one CEO told me during a workshop – "Chris, you are breaking my brain." It is far easier to defend old perspectives than embrace new ones, but unless we dare to think differently and explore new perspectives, we will never grow.

*Author and speaker **Christian Monö** has dedicated almost 20 years to exploring natural followership and its impact on individuals, organizations, and societies. His insights and expertise have been sought by clients ranging from universities to the Swedish Armed Forces.*

By Ira Chaleff

Followership, Courage and Intelligent Disobedience

You cannot have good followership without courage. Paradoxically, good leaders minimize the need for courage in their followers. Let's examine these premises.

Leading and following can and do occur outside the realm of hierarchy. For example, on the dance floor. Or amongst a group of friends with different interests and talents who take turns leading and following in social situations.

But most leading and following, and certainly that which occurs in business or government service, occur within the framework of hierarchy and power differential. The boss can hire, fire, promote, demote, issue orders and reverse them. The employee cannot.

Because of this reality, there is a formal power imbalance in favour of the leader. The balance is not entirely skewed, as a very talented employee who can take their services elsewhere, has their own source of power. But generally speaking, it is the employee – the follower - who experiences themselves as more vulnerable than the leader.

Given these dynamics, we find the follower needing to "read the boss" when approaching them with divergent ideas, requests that require signoff, desires for promotion or more favourable assignments or, most delicately, feedback on the boss' actions. Are they in a good mood? Are recent experiences likely to make them amenable to the conversation? Are they on solid footing with the leader or is it thin ice?

As has been correctly observed, courage is not the absence of fear but rather what is needed to act in the face of fear. Social courage is every bit as necessary as physical courage. We learn from Abraham Maslow that our social need to feel we belong is a strong motivator. Only when we feel secure in our relationships, do we

Most leading and following, and certainly that which occurs in business or government service, occur within the framework of hierarchy and power differential.

take risks to reach new levels of accomplishment and the self-esteem that accompanies this.

When we are working to develop followership skills, we want to identify and tap into our own sources of courage. This is what enables us to psychologically level the playing field with the formal leader. We are then more open to authentic conversation about what is needed for our success and that of the group.

What are the sources of courage? They are unique to our lived experience. For some it is a deep belief in doing what is right, based on our upbringing or religious convictions. For others it may be a role model from our own family, or a cultural icon whom we have admired. Still others rely on their professional reputation and wide network of supporters and allies. What is important is that we know how to find courage when we perceive risk to our personal safety.

Let's take an example.

We are a middle manager. This means we have two roles – one as a leader to those who report to us and one

> *Courage is not the absence of fear but rather what is needed to act in the face of fear.*

as a follower of the leader to whom we report. We find ourselves in a situation in which our capacity to lead our team is being undermined by the behaviour of our formal leader. They thoughtlessly give orders to our team, or make suggestions that are taken as orders, without going through us. This leaves us blindsided and repeatedly finding our team diverted from the plans and timelines we have carefully developed to meet our objectives.

We need to address this with the manager. Other unit heads have tried to do so and have been shot down. Some experienced subsequent retribution. This makes us anxious. We don't want to unnecessarily hurt our promotion prospects in this company. How do we proceed?

The manager has their attention on another priority – a critical deadline for a major customer. Our first move might be to give their priority extra attention, meeting the deadline to the customer's full satisfaction. Our manager's stress level lowers and they appreciate how we got our team to perform with flying colours. We have clearly been fully supportive. In a sense, we have earned the standing to now raise the sensitive management style issue.

There is still risk in the encounter. We know the manager does not accept upward feedback well. Nevertheless, if we are to continue to get good performance from our team and find satisfaction in our work, we need to bring up the issue and have it taken seriously. In this case our courage comes from wanting to buffer our team from conflicting orders that create confusion and resentment. It is our commitment to our team that gives us the courage to raise the matter with the manager.

We broach the matter skillfully, with good timing, and the manager is receptive. This is a good outcome. We found the courage and communicated effectively, despite the power differential. This is the skill set needed when we are in the follower role. But it required careful strategizing and taking a career risk to initiate the conversation. Not all our peers would be willing to do that. Many would harbour their resentment and give less of them-

Thank the team member sincerely for their willingness to bring their ideas and concerns. Never have them leave regretting that they tried.

selves to the success of the organization. No one "wins" in this state of affairs.

What could the leader do differently to *lower* the courage needed to raise sensitive matters with them? We have all heard leaders claim they have an "open door policy" and any of their team can come in and tell them anything they want. They believe this is sufficient to create a culture where their followers feel safe to do so. Usually, this is not the reality that their employees experience.

Some have taken up the manager on this invitation and found the experience painful. Before they were able to get out three sentences explaining the situation, the manager becomes defensive and refutes what they are saying, at times harshly or mockingly. Or they do listen politely, but then do nothing to remedy the matter. Their subordinates soon conclude there is no point in giving feedback. They stop doing so and grumble behind the manager's back, contributing to poor morale.

The manager has to be very intentional to create a truly psychologically safe space that invites and elicits constructive feedback. Their listening skills will need to be strong and authentic. When a team member does come in that door, they need to treat it as a test of their willingness to receive fresh ideas or feedback: give their full attention to the conversation; check they have correctly understood what they are being told; give the matter serious consideration.

They will need to be candid about which ideas they can and will act on, and then carry through with those. If they can't act on a specific matter, explain why and let that be the exception rather than the rule. Thank the team member sincerely for their willingness to bring their ideas and concerns. Never have them leave regretting that they tried.

The result is the manager creates a culture in which constructive, candid communication and feedback becomes a norm in the workplace. No special courage is required to speak up. Everyone understands that not every idea they bring will be acted on, but all will be seriously considered. None will be grounds for penalizing the employee. When the follower has helped the leader understand something of particular importance, this will be reflected in positive performance reviews. The manager may even publicly thank them at a staff meeting to reinforce the norms of the culture they are creating.

Be prepared to shift the lead and follow role and then shift back again when the situation is resolved. When this is understood, it translates well into organizational team dynamics.

Taking this one step further, there is also the option for the follower to exercise what is known as intelligent disobedience. This is the *sine qua non* of trust between leaders and followers.

The term "intelligent disobedience" comes from the training guide dogs receive when preparing to work with an individual who is blind. After learning to *obey* all the commands they need to know to assist the individual - who is their leader - they learn to *disobey* if obedience would result in harm to the leader or team. Clearly, this requires a high level of discernment by the guide dog and trust on the part of the leader.

Imagine that the leader and dog walk each morning to the train station for the commute into the city. The dog knows to stop and wait at each intersection until the leader gives the command to go forward. Normally this is routine. Last night, however, there was a wind storm. Tree branches have come down and are in their path.

When the leader gives the forward command, the dog disobeys even when the command is repeated. Though the leader can't see the obstacles, he trusts the dog and remains still.

Now the dog assumes the lead. It can easily jump over the branches or crawl under them, but it must make a decision that will keep the human in its charge safe. If it can find a clear path around the obstacles, it leads them on that route to their destination. If it cannot, it returns them safely home. Once the danger has been navigated, the human again assumes the lead.

Notice that both the human and the dog need to be cognizant of when intelligent disobedience is the appropriate response to a situation. Each needs to be prepared to shift the lead and follow role and then shift back again when the situation is resolved. When this is understood, it translates well into organizational team dynamics.

In November 2023, the British Army held a conference at the National Army Museum in London titled "Creating Effective Followership". The event marked the inclusion of a twenty page *Followership Note* to the *British Army Leadership Doctrine*. The discussions included an understanding of what courageous followership and exemplary followership mean at all levels of service. It also reviewed the subject of intelligent disobedience.

The panel on which I served included a former deputy chief medical officer of England, a retired Lt-Colonel, and a non-commissioned officer, WO 2, Adam Croucher. The audience was transfixed when the lowest ranking member of the panel, WO 2 Croucher, recounted an incident in the evacuation of Kabul, Afghanistan.

He and his unit were guarding a perimeter of the airport. Thousands of Afghans were threatening to break through the line, which would have overrun the base, blocking the further evacuation of personnel. Croucher received an order from his superior office who was stationed in a hangar, with limited vision of the reality

Organizational cultures are built by memorable acts at all levels of the organization - acts that come to represent how the organization views itself, what it values, and what it aspires to.

at the perimeter. The order was to pull his troops back into the hangar. Realizing this would lead to chaos, he told his unit to the hold the line while he hurried to the command centre in the hangar.

Once there, he told the officer who issued the order that his closed-circuit-tv view was not giving the full picture and asked him to come to the front line, which he did. He immediately saw that Croucher's assessment was correct and rescinded the order, resulting in a more orderly retreat at that location, while other locations experienced the full brunt of the panicked crowds. This was a classic example of intelligent disobedience on the junior officer's part, and appropriate responsiveness by the senior officer. Courage was needed in many ways that day, but not as much as would have been required in an inflexible command and control system.

Organizational cultures are built by memorable acts at all levels of the organization - acts that come to represent how the organization views itself, what it values, and what it aspires to. Courage will always be needed, as most human beings bring their early experiences with authority to their new groups. It is not immediately clear if loyal dissent or intelligent disobedience will be well received, or dealt with punitively. Leaders can accelerate the learning curve so their teams know it is safe to productively question what is coming down from the hierarchy, when doing so improves effectiveness and morale. Where leaders fail in this, followers can still find the courage to speak up in service of the mission and values.

Yes, there is a hierarchy in most leader-follower relations. There is also a dance that can be practiced and gracefully performed, at times to stunning effect. Whether you are the leader or the follower, invite your partners to join you.

Ira Chaleff is the best-selling author of The Courageous Follower *and* Intelligent Disobedience*, as well as the founder of the International Leadership Association's Followership Learning Community. He is a frequent speaker and workshop presenter on Courageous Followership, and was adjunct faculty at Georgetown University and visiting leadership scholar at The Möller Institute, Churchill College, Cambridge University.* **www.irachaleff.com**

By Langley Sharp MBE

The Reciprocity of Trust in High Performance Teams

Many of us may reflect on our professional careers and recall transformative moments, experiences so pivotal that they evoke visceral memories. One of my earliest occurred on a cold, wet, winter morning, in the rural county of Fermanagh, Northern Ireland. We had gathered in a dormitory-style room at one end of Enniskillen Police Station, a space no bigger than half a basketball court. To the people stood in front of me it was their home for six months, crammed in two rows of triple-high bunkbeds. This was 5 Platoon, B Company, 2 PARA. Standing there feeling somewhat exposed and trying desperately to exert an air of confidence, I was introduced as their new platoon commander. 30 seasoned paratroopers were now staring at me. The weight of judgement was palpable.

It was in that moment, fresh from 18 months of initial Army officer training, that the difference between command and leadership became a stark reality. I now had command authority of these young men, an authority with legal and constitutional status, and, as the Army's doctrine articulates, the responsibility and accountability that is implicit. I would ultimately be held accountable for not only the decisions and actions I took, but those of the soldiers before me. Yet, with the motto of The Royal Military Academy Sandhurst, *Serve to Lead,* ringing in my ears, I was also expected to be a leader. Whilst command is grounded in designated authority, leadership is a social relationship, a symbiotic partnership between leader and led.

One of the primary roles of any leader is to build this social relationship, nurturing the connections whose strength directly influences the collective performance of the group. It was acutely evident to me therefore, that to leverage the best of the talent and experience of the platoon, command authority would only get me so far. It

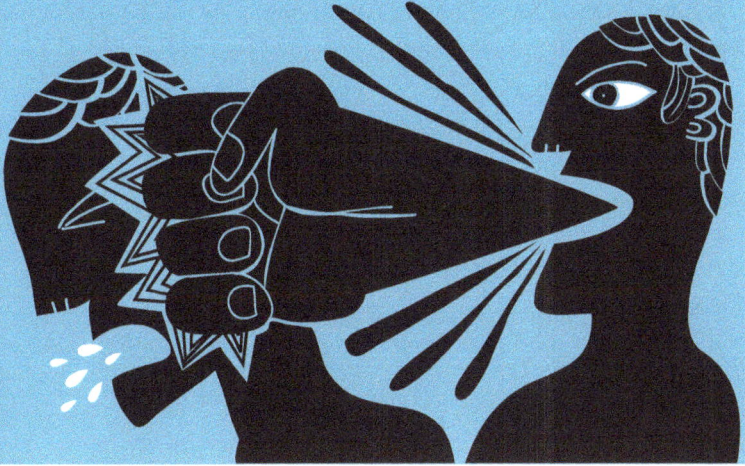

Authority is granted, leadership is earned.

was incumbent on me to develop relationships with every individual and to play my part in strengthening the social bonds of the team, upon which the mission depended. Authority is granted, leadership is earned.

But this is not just a tale of leadership. All too often, the focus of analysis is that of the man or woman 'out in front'. Far less the subject of study or debate is the effect such leaders create. Leaders may be the catalyst for change or action, but they are rarely the effect itself. That is the preserve of those who they seek to influence, the followers. As defined in the British Army's recently published Doctrine Note, followership is, 'the act of an individual or individuals willingly accepting the influence of others to achieve a shared outcome.' Key to this definition is willing acceptance, for, as the Note continues, followership, '…requires the consent of those being led, whether consciously or unconsciously. A leader appeals to the wants and needs of an individual and, in return, the individual assesses whether it is in their interest to assume the role of follower.'

Eight months after that individually seminal moment, the world shared a collectively defining experience in the terror attacks of 9/11, an event that was to irrevocably shape my service over the next two decades. Reflecting on a further eight operational tours, a decade in special forces and command at every level up to battalion, I was intrigued to understand what compels one to 'willingly follow'? What are the key ingredients to creating those social bonds and cementing relationships? Unlocking these provides not just the grounds for effective followership but great leadership and, in tandem, high performance. Having variously considered the compelling influences of authority, belonging, power and purpose, I consistently return to the essence of any credible partnership, trust.

But what is trust, why does it matter and how is the reciprocity of trust nurtured between leader and led?

A leader appeals to the wants and needs of an individual and, in return, the individual assesses whether it is in their interest to assume the role of follower.

The Fuel and the Glue (What and Why)

Like many well-versed but often nebulous business concepts, such as 'strategy', 'culture' and 'leadership' itself, trust is routinely touted as a fundamental to organizational success yet eludes universal understanding. Defined variously as 'a belief in the reliability of someone or something', trust is the cornerstone of our functioning as a social species, our ability to form relationships and to collaborate effectively. Indeed, hardwired to trust, our very survival demands it. We trust our parents and loved ones, our closest friends, our loyal teams and, to a greater or lesser extent, complete strangers. As Stephen Scott, founder of the behavioural analytics company Starling Trust argues, 'Our survival as a species has hinged on an ability to cooperate with trusted others.' Moreover, our domination as humankind has arguably been born not just of our superior intelligence but our ability to scale trust. 'Our thriving as a species has come as a conse-

Trust provides a binding function, a conscious, or often unconscious, commitment that an individual makes towards another on a judgement of perceived safety to one's own self interests.

quence of our ability to collaborate with strangers, at scale, as a presumed behavioral norm.' From interpersonal relationships and high-performing teams, to functioning nation states, trust is sacrosanct.

As US Army Lieutenant General Robert L. Caslen wrote, 'trust is both the fuel that drives the Army and the glue that holds it together.' In his simple statement, Caslen captures two critical facets of this all-pervasive concept. On the one hand, trust provides a binding function, a conscious, or often unconscious, commitment that an individual makes towards another on a judgement of perceived safety to one's own self interests. With cohesiveness established, trust also provides the 'fuel', enabling individuals to act effectively together. It allows us to challenge, innovate and make decisions in the interests of the group. Moreover, it is trust that unleashes the full potential of any team. Through this sense of assured reliability, we are able to grant agency

to others, who in turn seize responsibility for devolved decision-making and action. When people feel appropriately empowered, they are more motivated, accept greater ownership and add further value. Moreover, the organization is happier, healthier, and more productive. Trust, therefore, supports the two fundamental obligations of any business or organisation; the moral responsibility to look after its people and, inextricably linked, the corporate responsibility to optimise its core purpose.

But consistency in high performance requires a responsibility from every individual in the team. The very nature of trust is one of reciprocity, a mutual responsibility between leader and led (as well as peer-to-peer) to create, sustain and magnify. Followers need to trust that their leader will form sound judgements, share sacrifices, use their authority appropriately and act with integrity. In turn, leaders need to trust their followers to take ownership, be proactive within the given intent, and provide candid feedback. As I stated in the Army's official account of leadership, *The Habit of Excellence,* 'Without these layers of vertical and horizontal trust, communication breaks down, confidence ebbs and mission success is threatened.' This leader-follower reciprocity demands what I refer to as the '5 Cs of Trust': competency, consistency, character, courage and care.

The 5 Cs of Trust (How)
Competency
First and foremost, trust is earned through a perception of role-specific competency. From close friends to complete strangers, it is arguably one of the primary metrics of judging whether to trust. We trust a pilot to fly us, a dentist to drill our teeth and teachers to care for our children. Yet competence is contextual. A surgeon might be trusted to conduct a life-saving operation but not to build a house extension. We trust those we deem to have the relevant skills and experience expected of their position, and necessary for the task in hand.

Beyond task-specific technical skills, leaders are also prized for their competency in decision-making. Problem analysis, judgement and clear communication are staple expectations of leadership competency. Yet in a fast-evolving world, many leaders are challenged to keep pace with the breadth and depth of specialist skills required to remain competitive. Whilst a growth mindset is important for any leadership role, increasingly those in senior positions find themselves at the behest of the knowledge of those more junior. Having the humility to know when others should step forward and assume the leader role, regardless of formal positions of authority, are a fast-track to earning trust and respect. In my first few months on operations, I routinely deferred to my soldiers and junior leaders to contribute their superior experience to the plans that I would ultimately direct. Almost 20 years later I commanded a Parachute Regiment battalion. Despite the wealth of experience I had accumulated, almost on a daily basis I would revert to the role of follower in favour of those more junior to me, on the grounds of competency. Not only was it right for the task, but it undoubtedly enhanced mutual trust and respect.

But trust is reciprocal. For followers to earn their leader's trust they too must demonstrate the competencies expected of their role, to consistently push boundaries, take the initiative and assume ownership of their part in the collective endeavours. High performing teams thrive on the delegation of responsibility that enables

Having the humility to know when others should step forward and assume the leader role, regardless of formal positions of authority, are a fast-track to earning trust and respect.

everyone to offer their full potential. Yet delegation comes at risk to those enabling it. First and foremost, leaders need to be reassured that granting agency to others will be met by a competency to deliver. As the British Army's doctrine succinctly states:

> '*Followers feel and believe in the imperative of mutual trust in both the leader-follower and commander-subordinate relationship. As much as they expect their leader to trust them, they ensure reciprocal trust by being loyal, selflessly committed, reliable and values-driven, as well as consistently delivering to the highest standards.*'

Consistency

As former Deputy Chairman of Saatchi and Saatchi, Richard Hytner put simply, 'People like to know they can trust you, and trust is predictable behaviour over time.' By nature we crave certainty; certainty reassures. From individuals to institutions, we trust those we can predict: doctors with a track record of successful patient care; investment funds routinely yielding high returns; and e-commerce companies delivering on time and at speed. In the same way we might access the validity of data based on patterns of predictability, so too do we assess trust in others based on predictability of their actions. We seek consistency in competency – in the performance, product or service delivered – but also in character. We trust others because we know what they stand for and that they are consistent in acting in accordance with their shared values.

Trust is rapidly eroded if those deemed close allies of the leader are treated more favourably. A perceived lack of moral courage in failing to maintain standards for all is a secured path to undermining credibility. Consistency in behaviour is also a foundation of effective followership, generating trust from both leaders and peers alike. Leaders are more likely to invest responsibility and freedom to act in those they are assured will deliver.

Consistency is a cumulative effect. It is the predictability of everyday actions built-up over time. Hence why elite team performance is matured with leaders, peers and followers alike having developed an almost intuitive understanding of one another's behaviours. When it matters most therefore, on the battlefield, pitch or boardroom, the very best teams are able to act on instinct.

Regardless of the uncertainty and volatility of the situation, trust is implicit based on consistent, predictable behaviours.

Character

Acclaimed WWII General and former Chief of Staff of the US Army, Matthew Ridgway once stated, 'Character is the bedrock on which the whole edifice of leadership rests. Without it, particularly in the military profession, failure in peace, disaster in war, or, at best, mediocrity in both will result.'

Tactical mistakes he could abide, often using them as a vehicle for our development, but behavioural transgressions or poor moral judgements would face a harsher critic.

In this succinct yet powerful statement, Ridgway encapsulated the essence of why trust matters. We trust others because we have faith in who they are – their character. Defined as 'the mental and moral qualities distinctive to an individual,' character might otherwise be seen as the 'true you'. It is, as Mary Crossan et al. described, the 'interconnected set of habituated patterns of thought, emotion, motivation or volition, and action,' that reflect what is deemed to be virtuous. In those regarded as being of trustworthy character, there is not only a consistency and alignment of thoughts, words and deeds, but all are judged to be virtuous. Put simply, we trust those who demonstrate integrity, knowing they will do the right thing in difficult circumstances.

In my first six months as a platoon commander, I benefitted from the mentorship of our highly respected company commander, Major Rob Stephenson. Not only was he the consummate professional but expected, and role modelled, high moral standards. Tactical mistakes

Courage is also required to let go of control, passing the baton to others even if the assigned leader remains ultimately accountable.

he could abide, often using them as a vehicle for our development, but behavioural transgressions or poor moral judgements would face a harsher critic. It was an early lesson in securing and maintaining trust. If the 'easy' decisions were taken in peacetime when the stakes were low, the implications for such habitual decision-making in war could be catastrophic. Hence for the British Army, adherence to its Values and Standards – the moral boundaries that inform expected standards of behaviour for both leaders and followers alike – is paramount. As author James Kerr stated, 'Our values decide our character. Our character decides our value.'

Courage

'Courage,' C.S. Lewis would argue, 'is not simply one of the virtues, but the form of every virtue at the testing point, which means at the point of highest reality.' It is of little surprise therefore, that courage is considered *primus inter pares* amongst British Army values. Not just the physical courage required to deliver its core purpose, but the moral courage to do so within the expectations of the society it serves.

But both as leader and follower, courage, a psychological tenacity borne of true inner confidence, manifests in many forms. We trust leaders with the courage to make difficult decisions, to stay the course amid uncertainty, and to hold both themselves and others to account in the maintenance of high standards. Courage is also required to let go of control, passing the baton to others even if the assigned leader remains ultimately accountable.

Furthermore, it takes courage to be vulnerable. As Patrick Lencioni advocates in *Five Dysfunctions of a Team*, it is vulnerability-based trust that drives true performance. The courage to self-identify and declare '...skill deficiencies, interpersonal shortcomings and requests for help.' Often perceived as a weakness, vulnerability, when applied with contextual judgement, is a strength. It allows others to see the human side of a leader and in so doing, gives permission for others to mimic, encouraging a far more open and transparent environment. This creates what Professor Amy Edmondson terms *psychological safety,* 'a shared belief held by members of a team that the team is safe for interpersonal risk taking.' It is such risk-taking that drives much-heralded creativity and innovation, providing people the cognitive and

The role of the leader is to serve the interests of those they have the privilege to lead.

emotional latitude to 'intelligently fail.' It also promotes a healthy but too often elusive challenge culture, in which people have the courage to disagree, question traditional thinking and provide alternative perspectives. It is in such an environment, rooted in courage, that real progress is made. As the Army Doctrine Note states, 'Without challenge, failures are not learnt from, groupthink is reinforced, safety compromised, cognitive diversity suppressed, initiative stifled, and homogeneity fostered.'

But such a culture of risk-taking and challenge encouraged by the leader is not realized if courage is not reciprocated by followers. They too face demands to do the right thing, admit mistakes and persevere in difficult times. But they must also have the courage to speak with candour in the interests of the task. In the parallel and complementary rank structure of the Army, the role of the Non-Commissioned Officer (NCO) is often vital in this regard. At the interface of turning direction into action, NCOs are entrusted to speak 'truth to power,' ensuring that higher-level decision-making matches tactical reality. Courageous NCOs, acting as critical friends, have been at the heart of every effective military team I

have worked with. Those most respected are unabashed in offering honest, purposeful challenge, based on a mutually trusting relationship that relies on what Timothy R, Clark defines as 'high intellectual friction and low social friction.' A challenge culture, underpinned by the courage of leaders and followers alike, is an undoubted competitive advantage.

Care

In 1945, three years after taking command of the Four-teenth Army, Field Marshal Viscount Slim led what many regard as one of the finest victories in military history. Turning 'defeat into victory' in the jungles of Burma, he reversed the fortunes of a ravaged million-strong multi-national force, to vanquish the revered Japanese Impe-rial Army. Affectionally known as 'Uncle Bill', Slim was renowned on the one hand as a leader with a sharp decisive mind, a willingness to take calculated risks and driven by an indomitable will to win, and, on the other, great humility, an advocacy for empowered action, and a deeply held love and respect for his soldiers. From senior generals to junior soldiers, Slim was universally trusted because he cared.

This innate desire to be protected, valued and loved, stems from one of the most natural of human instincts. Our survival necessitates a sense of safety and we feel safe in the hands of those we believe will look after our interests. In turn, we trust. The role of the leader, there-fore, is to serve the interests of those they have the priv-ilege to lead. As Major General Patrick Marriott, former Commandant of The Royal Military Academy Sand-hurst argues, 'That preparedness to serve others at the expense of oneself is perhaps one of the litmus tests by which others judge leaders – and quite rightly.' Caring for

For teams to perform at their best, service to others cannot be the preserve of the leader alone. Followers must have an equal commitment to the interests of their leaders and teammates alike.

others requires leaders to know their people, to understand their motivations, appreciate their strengths and weaknesses, and support their aspirations. It demands an intention that goes beyond the needs of the task, or expectations of the team and focuses on the intimate needs of every individual. As President Roosevelt wisely counselled, 'Nobody cares how much you know until they know how much you care.'

Assured that the leader cares, followers trust, and with such trust comes a reciprocal expectation of loyalty and compassion. For teams to perform at their best, service to others cannot be the preserve of the leader alone. Followers must have an equal commitment to the interests of their leaders and teammates alike. Phil Jackson, one of the most successful basketball coaches of all time, understood this intuitively. 'Good teams become great ones when the members trust each other enough to surrender the "me" for the "we".'

Summary

It is this sense of service to the "we" not the "me" that has defined my military experience. From the 30 paratroopers who first helped to mould me into the leader and follower I was to become, to the many thousands I have had the privilege of both leading and being led by since, it was selfless service that united us. The intense social connections developed, akin to familial love at their strongest, were the catalyst for us to operate, and succeed, in the most extreme of environments, amid the most daunting of challenges. The result was a force-multiplying effect far beyond the capabilities of any one individual. For success, whether in business, sport or public service, is a collective endeavour.

Yet true teamship cannot be realized without the 'fuel and glue' of trust. Trust is the currency of high performance, strengthening and scaling the social bonds we reply upon to operate at the highest level. It is hard fought and easily lost, demanding responsibility from every individual. Enduring success requires an intricate web of symbiotic and mutually reinforcing partnerships, every individual engaged in a reciprocity of trust. It is the '5 Cs of Trust' – competency, consistency, character, courage and care – that unlock both great leadership and effective followership, and in tandem, exceptional team performance.

A fully referenced version of this article is available on request from editor@dl-q.com

Langley Sharp MBE *is the former head of the Centre for Army Leadership, responsible for championing leadership excellence across the British Army. He led a counter-insurgency Task Force operation, commanded a Parachute Regiment Battalion and delivered the training programme for the London 2012 Olympics venue security, for which he was awarded an MBE. He is the author of the British Army's official account of leadership,* The Habit of Excellence.

By Basil Read

Levels of Empowerment

How Followership is Changing the Leader-Follower Dynamic

While follower or employee empowerment is a 21st Century knowledge age buzzword, old industrial age paradigms of the leader-follower dynamic persist. In many parts of today's globalized society people are still caught up in what has been described as the romance of leadership, where all the successes or failures of an organization are attributed to the leader. This placing of the leader on a pedestal neglects the very real contributions that followers make to organizational outcomes.

The persistence of this understanding of the leader-follower dynamic traces its roots back to the first industrial revolution in 18th Century England. The harnessing of steam power fueled a transition from an agricultural society and individual artisans to an early form of factory labour. In the factory system, labourers performed a set of repetitive tasks under the watchful eye of a supervisor who had overall responsibility for output and quality control. While these early factories largely involved large numbers of individual contributors or small teams as compared to the assembly lines of the second industrial revolution, the first revolution set in motion a senior-subordinate dynamic where the supervisor was given credit for the output and quality of the workmanship. While some might argue that the European artisan guild system was similar, the apprentice-to-journeyman-to-master sequence provided an equal opportunity for advancement to master, whereas the factory system offered little opportunity for career progression to a leader position.

This supervisor-subordinate (leader-follower) relationship was further codified by Fredrick Taylor's early 20th Century studies on time and efficiency and the exposure of millions of men to the top-down command and control structure of the military, particularly during World Wars One and Two.

A central characteristic of the knowledge age economy is that workers tend to be hired more for their brain power than their physical power (manual dexterity). This has real implications for the leader-follower dynamic as leaders move from their traditional oversight function to coordination and the follower role shifts from automaton to an empowered subject matter expert.

Command and control proved to be an ideal form of efficient production with workers performing machine-like tasks that typically required little more than muscle memory. Ford's automobile assembly line, introduced in 1913, is a case in point with workers performing the same repetitive task over-and-over during an 8-hour shift. While serving as a hallmark of the industrial age, and still in use today, command and control systems in organizations are giving way to the networked systems of the knowledge age which require a different leader-follower dynamic.

Followership in the Knowledge Age

Many scholars mark the 1990s as the beginning of the knowledge age where global economies shifted from an

Both empowerment given by the leader and follower self-empowerment enhance productivity and mission effectiveness.

industrial base to a knowledge base. A central characteristic of the knowledge age economy is that workers tend to be hired more for their brain power than their physical power (manual dexterity). This has real implications for the leader-follower dynamic as leaders move from their traditional oversight function to coordination and the follower role shifts from automaton to an empowered subject matter expert. This is not to suggest that throughout the ages there have not been leader-coordinators or followers possessing unique knowledge and skill. Rather the demands of the age, including increased reliance on information technology and a globalized environment, has produced a greater need for coordinating rather than supervising the efforts of followers who are or should be empowered decision-makers.

At the dawn of this new age, scholars such as Robert Kelley and Ira Chaleff began to offer a new narrative of the follower role. While acknowledging that some could continue to follow the leader in a passive sheeplike manner, Kelley and Chaleff argued that followers have a vital role to play in organizational success. Further, Chaleff holds that followers have a duty to help their leader stay on track. To this end he advocates for follow-

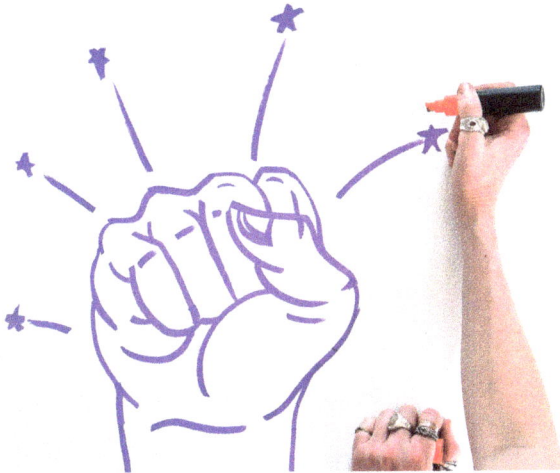

ers partnering with the leader to achieve organizational goals. But in doing so, the follower must balance being supportive with a willingness to respectfully challenge their leader when the leader's actions or behaviours detract from mission achievement.

Empowerment and Followership

Both scholars and authors in the practitioner space have long advocated for employee empowerment as a means of improving productivity and enhancing mission achievement. Empowerment may be given by the leader to leverage follower knowledge, skills and abilities, or assumed by the follower who envisions him or herself as an owner of the mission. Both empowerment given by the leader and follower self-empowerment enhance productivity and mission effectiveness as seen in the cases below.

Followership Through Leader/Organization Empowerment – The NUMMI Case

New United Motor Manufacturing Incorporated (NUMMI) was a joint venture between US car manufacturer General Motors (GM) and Japan's Toyota Motor Corporation that operated at the former GM Fremont California plant from 1984 to 2010. While, as noted above, scholars often mark the beginning of the knowledge age as somewhere in the 1990s it had a much earlier start in some sectors in Japan, most notably in the automobile industry.

Japan's automobile industry was heavily influenced by the post WWII teachings of W. Edwards Deming, an American quality control expert. Demings' concept of *total quality control* (also called total quality management) stresses that the skills and competencies of all employees must be honoured and followers have an obligation to speak up to management in pursuit of best practices and behaviours that lead to mission success. For example, at Toyota, an employee in pursuit of the organization's mission of producing a quality product may stop the entire assembly line at any time, without management permission.

In empowering its employees, Toyota leveraged the Japanese concept of *nemawashi*; a term that engages all involved in a particular process in solving problems and consensus building; i.e. working together to identify and implement solutions. These empowerment measures led to improved productivity, efficiency and a high level of product quality; something American automobile manufactures desired to implement in their production facilities.

In an effort to replicate Toyota's success both in quality and productivity, GM partnered with Toyota in 1984 to reopen its shuttered Freemont California factory. The Freemont plant had been plagued by high employee absenteeism, substance abuse, low quality vehicle assembly and uneven productivity. As noted in an interview with a United Auto Workers (UAW) leader Bruce Lee, the Freemont plant was the worst in the nation resulting in its closure two years before the start of NUMMI.

The NUMMI venture began with a combined Toyota/GM management team, with Toyota executives in the CEO and COO positions. As the factory worked towards reopening, and for some time thereafter, groups of employees were sent to Japan to learn "the Toyota way". The Toyota way includes an expectation that every employee from top brass to recent hires, should "be looking for ways to improve the production process all the time, to make the workers' job easier and more efficient". This meant that Toyota employees are empowered to critically critique processes, be they mechanical, physical or behavioural, and offer suggestions for improvement.

The Toyota way includes an expectation that every employee from top brass to recent hires should "be looking for ways to improve the production process all the time, to make the workers' job easier and more efficient".

Taking back their lessons learned from Japan, UAW workers at the NUMMI plant staged a remarkable turnaround of the Freemont plant. Within a few years, NUMMI had become the best performing automobile plant in the United States. Known for high quality workmanship, efficiency and productivity, largely as a result of empowering its employees NUMMI presented the American auto industry with a better manufacturing environment. While GM took many of the lessons-learned from the joint experiment and applied them to other facilities around the country, unfortunately NUMMI did not survive the meltdown of the US auto industry during the Great Recession.

The FDIC Case – Followership Through Self-Empowerment

In 2014 the author discussed the 2009 introduction of followership education at the US Federal Deposit Insurance Corporation (FDIC) as part of its culture change initiative. As a component of a larger shift to a holistic approach to leadership development within the agency, instruction in followership was delivered as one of several initiatives designed to increase employee empowerment, mission ownership and engagement with leaders. One of the unique benefits of incorporating followership into the culture change initiative was its focus on the follower initiating a partnering relationship with the leader and giving the follower a voice in helping the leader make wise decisions.

As a banking regulator, nearly half of the FDIC's workforce are bank supervision and compliance examiners who work out of field offices spread across the United States. Teams of examiners are deployed to banks within each field office's territory on a periodic schedule to examine the health of each assigned institution and its compliance with various government policies and regulations. Leadership of these teams rotates amongst the office's commissioned examiners; meaning that an individual who was in charge of an examination at one institution may be the follower of someone she has previously led a few weeks or months later. This rotational scheme, coupled with each examiner's age, experience, gender, etc., creates a myriad of leader-follower dynamics. At the FDIC, it just as common for younger examiners to lead a team that has members with more experience as it is for a very experienced examiner to lead a team of newer employees. Thus, FDIC's rotating leader-follower role in the examiner workforce provides a unique follower-ship opportunity that promotes the partnering dynamic regardless of position.

While the FDIC promotes the concept of leaders empowering employees throughout the organization, instruction in followership across all levels of the agency provides employees, to include leaders who follow other leaders, the skills necessary for self-empowerment. As one graduate of the Introduction to FDIC Leadership course noted, "it's not enough for me to wait to be told to do something. I have to say what needs to be done to my manager". This sentiment of feeling self-empowered to take ownership enables the follower to act in the best interests of the organization's mission and when neces-sary, go beyond the limits of the empowerment provided by the leader. As Marc and Samanatha Hurwitz have noted "people [who are] immersed in followership devel-opment ... see it as empowering ... and that agency is not the sole purview of those with formal leadership titles".

One of the unique benefits of incorporating followership into the culture change initiative was its focus on the follower initiating a partnering relationship with the leader and giving the follower a voice in helping the leader make wise decisions.

FDIC's engagement in followership education and training was a small part of the agency's overall culture change initiative. Yet as seen in the quotes above the self-empowerment aspect of followership contributed to the overall effort; resulting in the FDIC moving from near last to being named the best place to work among mid-sized agencies in the Federal government. A position it held for several years.

Knowledge and Empowerment

In the knowledge age competitive advantage is achieved through agile and creative employees operating in a collaborative environment where both leaders and followers are engaged in and have ownership of the mission. For followers to fully engage they must be empowered.

As seen in the NUMMI case, Japanese auto manufacturers have long held a significant share of the market as every employee is an empowered knowledge worker

> "My entire life I was led to believe that being a follower meant to be a static character in an organization ... now I know that it is far from static and actually one of the most dynamic roles in an organization".

focused on making constant improvements in support of the mission.. While management empowering employees can lead to powerful results, there may be limits placed on what followers are empowered to do. When, as seen at the FDIC, employees receive followership education and training, they are better able to partner with the leader because they are self-empowered and therefore unconstrained in their actions that support the mission. As another FDIC employee said following participation in followership training, "my entire life I was led to believe that being a follower meant to be a static character in an organization ... now I know that it is far from static and actually one of the most dynamic roles in an organization".

In the first three decades of the knowledge age our understanding of work has moved from largely being the province of physical labor to mental agility, yet many workplaces still adhere to old leader-follower models. A management system of empowering followers to act in certain situations, such as seen in the NUMMI case, benefits the overall organizational mission. Yet developing individual skill in followership, like the FDIC did fifteen years ago, frees the knowledge age follower to an unconstrained level of empowerment with the potential of achieving even higher levels of mission achievement.

A fully referenced version of this article is available by request from editor@dl-q.com

Basil Read III *was a US Navy Captain until 2007. He was Dean of Leadership Development at FDIC for 10 years from 2009. Today he is a leadership consultant, with a specific focus on followership.*

https://www.linkedin.com/in/j-basil-read-iii-ph-d-a1274b23/

By Julie Newman

A Followership Journey

A Human Resources Perspective on the Organization-Wide Implementation of a Leadership-Followership Program

Organizational Context

The year is 2019 and the worldwide COVID-19 pandemic is not yet on the horizon. Carizon Family and Community Services (a Mental Health and Wellbeing Non Profit of approximately 200 employees, based in Kitchener-Waterloo, Ontario) had been unified for over 5 years, but leadership was only just getting to the pieces that really mattered to our employees, our people. We had received feedback that Carizon's culture was undefined, that our

If the message was 'how to get people to do what we say' a quick exit would be implemented.

people wanted to have more input and folks wanted to know how their work was directly impacting the Kitchener-Waterloo community. Leadership was committed to an engagement journey with our people and in 2018-19 there was the opportunity to create a four-year strategic plan to effectively deliver critical services to the community. We kicked off our strategic planning with our people – an intentional choice to demonstrate that our people were a critical stakeholder in the process. This employee engagement continued throughout our planning whereby additional thoughts and ideas were brought back for our people's feedback. At the end of the process, we had a strategic plan that our people could easily communicate and recognize their essential contribution. There were four strategic directions:

- Build Carizon Culture
- Innovate to improve the customer experience
- Promote system change through collaboration
- Deepen our Family Focus

Everyone in the organization could speak to and was invested in this new plan.

Why Followership?

As the Director of Talent, Engagement & Quality, I had several deliverables in our first year of the strategic plan – most of them falling under the direction of "build Carizon culture". A key first step was to select a leadership model, but this was easier said than done. A number of potential models were explored, and options were shared with our leadership team. Their feedback was incorporated into our further search. Several models had great components, but nothing felt quite right. As the search continued, one of our contacts shared that she was a graphic recorder for an upcoming local conference that aligned with our general approach. It was the first annual Global Followership Conference.

Tracy Elop, Carizon's CEO and I decided to attend and see what "followership" was all about. Neither one of us knew what to expect but hoped that the conference message was not focused on how to get people to do what we say; if this was the message, a quick exit a would be implemented at the first opportunity. Fortunately, the message was nothing of the sort and a possible 'fit' seemed likely. Many folks in academia shared the potential benefits of followership along with a handful of consultants. It was fascinating. Samantha and Marc Hurwitz, authors of *Leadership is Half the Story, A Fresh Look at Followership, Leadership, and Collaboration*,

explained everyone is both a leader AND a follower. This concept was experienced through Sharna Fabiano's (author of Lead & Follow and host of Lead & Follow Podcast) experiential session that applied tango dance/movement to demonstrate how this worked in practice. The more we learned, the more this model appeared viable for Carizon. What stronger message of valuing your people could be sent than "all of you are leaders, and all of you are followers". This concept worked for every single person in our organization – from the CEO to our frontline specialized employees who directly interact with clients. It just fit.

Instead of trying to combat the stigma of "followership" we gave folks the training that non-management employees are rarely offered.

How did we do it?

And so, discussions with Samantha and Marc Hurwitz were initiated and a mini pilot of their program in our organization was designed to see whether this model was as great a fit for Carizon as we thought (remember, we were on an engagement journey). Our pilot group consisted of folks from various levels and departments to create a group that was representative of the organization. In true leadership-followership fashion we worked collaboratively with Samantha and Marc to share some key pieces of the model with the pilot group. The pilot was an overwhelming success, and the leadership-followership model would be implemented across the organization.

Carizon collaborated with FLiP University, Samantha and Marc's business, to customize an approach and strategy that would align with our organization. Historically, followership training was delivered first and was followed by leadership training. One of the challenges with offering followership training is that you need folks "buy-in" to followership right away. Being on an

We modelled a leadership-followership approach by completing the activity with our leadership team before asking them to complete it with their teams.

engagement journey, Carizon was concerned about what it would say to our employees, indirectly, if we started with followership training (ie we need you to do what we say, so we are going to give you training on how to do that). Instead, Carizon took a different approach and delivered leadership training first. Leadership training is what employees recognized and wanted. It worked incredibly well! Instead of trying to combat the stigma of "followership" we gave folks the training that non-management employees are rarely offered. Within the leadership training, they were introduced to the concept of followership and how it is critical for a leader to be easy to follow. When the time came to deliver followership training, it was just the natural next step in the training program and was well accepted by our people. Similarly, the delivery of Karen B.K. Chan's Emotional Intelligence training that followed followership training was also well accepted. Given Carizon is a mental health organization that employs skilled mental health professionals, it was anticipated that some of our employees would not see the value in emotional intelligence training as they would have had exposure to this type of material through their education. We were delighted and surprised to receive positive feedback from highly experienced professionals on how beneficial this training was.

The implementation of the leadership-followership program was carefully considered. An in-person kick-off meeting was the initial step and carried out at our next All Staff Event. The the leadership-followership model was introduced and discussed with our people. Employees completed online micro-trainings and interacted with a group of their peers through discussion forums and activities. This was reinforced with monthly activities, to support embedding leadership-followership training into our culture. We even modelled a leadership-followership approach by completing the activity with our leadership team before asking them to complete it with their teams. Care was taken throughout the process to ensure that our employees could see our commitment to leadership-followership and how this could be implemented into their daily routine.

What was the Outcome?

Carizon was on an engagement journey and the leadership-followership model provided a natural framework for our organisation. Carizon was dedicated to our people and to building a supportive and thriving organizational culture. Organizational values were co-created – ones that our employees would REMEMBER and live by. Quarterly pulse surveys were implemented, and we worked hard to make and communicate changes that would support our people. Followership was a piece of the puzzle that complemented and enhanced our work. It recognized the critical input of all our employees in successful evolution.

Our employees could see the value in receiving leadership and followership training and could envision changes that would happen once the model was fully embedded into our organization. Figure 1 shares some of our employees' reflections on what successful implementation of the leadership-followership program would look like. When you consider the impact from all of Carizon's efforts, we experienced an increase in our employee net promoter score from approximately 13 in June 2019 when our annual plan was launched to 41 by January 2021. The Leadership-Followership model provided Carizon with a framework and language that could be used throughout the organization. Samantha and Marc's analogy of leaders "set the frame" while "followers create within it" was frequently repeated. This allowed our leaders and our individual contributors to have clearer roles

Figure 1

Employee's Reflections of a Successful Leadership-Followership Program

Prior to commencing training, Employee's were asked "what does the success of the Leadership-Followership Program look like to you?" Employee's shared the following:

- "Being able to apply leadership skills to areas of my life where it may not have been thought possible in the past."

- "A more empowered workforce, with ideas and leadership happening in every direction."

- "All levels of employees feel listened to and valued no matter what their position/title."

- "Increased personal confidence, increased collaboration and cohesion, increased opportunities, new ideas and initiatives."

- "More balance between leaders and followers (more decisions made at the "ground" level)"

- "More autonomy for non leadership staff. A more meaningful division of workload between leadership and staff. More trust from leadership toward staff in respect to their capacity to successfully navigate challenging issues and affect change."

- "Feeling comfortable taking lead on something without feeling I HAVE to lead but also feeling comfortable following."

> *There is a stigma with respect to being a "follower" despite follower contributions being vital. There is great work and advocacy being done with the focus on changing this, but the perception that being a leader is more desirable than being a follower continues to persist.*

and understand how their own individual contributions made a difference. After completing the training, the question remained 'how frequently would our employees apply their leadership and followership training'? Employees reported that their leadership and followership skills were used almost equally. 71% reported using leadership skills weekly or daily while 75% reported using followership skills weekly or daily. Additionally, employees shared that they had the opportunity to demonstrate leadership in their current role almost 70% of the time.

As the formal training concluded, attention was redirected to embed leadership-followership into our organizational activities. For example, leadership and followership related interview questions were incorporated into our interview tools and our annual performance check-in questions. We also began working on organizational competencies including example

behaviours that would further embed leadership-followership into the organization.

What did we learn? What would we do differently?

Selecting a leadership-followership model in 2019 naturally aligned with Carizon's work. If you think about the alignment between leadership, followership, and authentic employee engagement, adopting a leadership-followership model provides a framework to naturally engage your people through your daily interactions. Complemented by a strong strategic plan and transportable values the leadership-followership model also supported Carizon in co-creating a thriving organizational culture. Leadership-Followership was a choice that not only complemented Carizon's other initiatives, but also enhanced them. Thinking back on our implementation there are two key takeaways worth highlighting:

Using the online training and supplementing it with in-person training and activities ... sends the strong unspoken commitment to your people: "you are investing in them".

1.   *Deliver Leadership Training First*

There is a stigma with respect to being a "follower" despite follower contributions being vital. There is great work and advocacy being done with the focus on changing this, but the perception that being a leader is more desirable than being a follower contin-ues to persist. The decision to deliver leadership training first to all employees across the organization allowed us to create excitement and receive buy-in from our employees right away. Perhaps it was also re-assuring that everyone (even our leaders) would receive innovative followership training as well? We feel very strongly that this order of the trainings was instrumental in the program's success.

2. *Train Everyone but Think Carefully About When*

Often in organizations leadership training is provided to only a select few. Training EVERYONE in both leadership and followership models was a key piece of our success. One is not better than the other and they are two distinct skill sets. Using the online training and supplementing it with in-person training and activities to embed learning is affordable and customizable to your organization. It also sends the very strong unspoken commitment to your people: "you are investing in them". During our implementation we experienced several challenges. We initially had a timeline to complete leadership, followership, and emotional intelligence training in one year. As an organization that has commitments to the community it serves, this proved to be challenging. We problem solved by extending some timelines and setting aside time in team meetings to complete the training for teams that had limited flexibility to complete the training independently during their regular workday.

As a non-profit in the mental health sector, one of the challenges we face is high turnover particularly in employees that are just entering the mental health field. Sometimes the field is not exactly what they expect, or folks get experience and move on to

Introducing formal training after a year or two of service would be a more sustainable and cost-effective approach.

other growth opportunities external to the organization. When we rolled out leadership-followership across the organization, we committed to training everyone – relief /casual workers, contract employees, part-time employees, etc. New employees were also introduced to the training right away. This was a large investment in our people. In hindsight, it would have been better to provide some guidelines with respect to when the training was introduced to ensure an ROI. For example, we learned that we lost employees that had been working for us less than 2 years at a much higher rate than any other employee group. However, we do not feel the leadership-followership training was contributing factor to this. Giving a general introduction to leadership-followership and the language commonly used as part of orientation would provide new employees with the needed information to understand leadership-followership at a high level. Introducing formal training after completing a year or two years of service would be a more sustainable and cost-effective approach.

Why should you consider implementing a Followership Program in your Organization?

The way of work has changed yet organizations continue to use traditional approaches. Training only leadership level employees impacts a very small percentage of your workforce compared to training your entire organization. Training everyone in the organization creates a significant improvement and with modern learning methodologies this can be affordable.

Organizations increasingly face complex challenges and according to McLean & Company, (the HR research firm's 2024 HR report, the top three HR challenges are recruiting top talent, providing a great employee experience, and controlling costs. Well executed implementation of a followership program can address all three of these top challenges. Phillip Podsakoff and Scott MacKenzie, professors at the Kelley School of Business, who focus on organizational citizenship behaviour,found that followership is linked to improvements of 17-43% of almost every single key organizational performance metric? Followership may very well be a key solution that has broad positive impacts for your organization. With the increased complexity and number of challenges organizations face, can you afford not to implement a followership program?

Where Did this Journey Lead?

In the non-profit sector, you are constantly looking to see how you can improve support to the community you serve while more effectively utilizing resources to improve service delivery. Carizon demonstrated this in 2013 when it became the new amalgamated entity of two smaller non-profits. In April 2023, Carizon did this once more when Carizon, KW-Counselling Services, and Monica Place unified to become Camino Mental Health + Wellbeing. The process of unifying (note the language of unification rather than take over or acquisition) in non-profits is quite different to that in the private sector. A great deal of care is taken around language as well as creating something that feels different from any of the originating organizations. This means that many initiatives get put on hold as the new organization considers the path they will forge to their future. For Camino, this meant taking a true leadership-followership approach by listening to its followers before deciding the next step in Camino's leadership journey.

__Julie Newman__ is a Certified Human Resources Leader, an HR educator, and the Founder and Principal for Willow Hall HR (Kitchener, Waterloo, Canada), an HR consulting firm that specializes in strategic HR for small and medium sized businesses. https://www.willowhallhr.com/

My followership journey at Carizon connected me with fellow HR professional, Debra Finlayson, which has inspired the two of us to collaborate as we continue to share our followership stories and expertise with other HR practitioners.

References:

M. Hurwitz and S. Hurwitz. Leadership is Half the Story: A Fresh Look at Followership, Leadership, and Collaboration. University of Toronto Press. Toronto. 2015.

Podsakoff, P.M., & MacKenzie, S.B. (1997). Impact of organizational citizenship behavior on organizational performance: A review and suggestions for future research. Human Performance, 10(2), 133-151.

McLean & Company. (2024). HR Trends Report: What Trends are making waves in 2024? Retrieved at: https://tinyurl.com/2jncpzbp

By Mark McCartney

To Pause and Reflect – The Leadership Imperative in Times of Change

A Perspective from a Sabbatical in South America

My fourteen year old son and I wrapped our arms around a 3,500 year old larch tree in Pumalin National Park in Chile. The park was made possible due to the visionary, Doug Tomkins, American businessman and conservationist.

My wife and I and our two sons walked across the Perito Moreno Glacier in Argentina. The guide told us that it takes 500 years from the snow falling in the high Andes to when giant chunks of ice calve and fall into the milky blue glacial lake below.

These two encounters encapsulate our exploration of natural wonders in South America experienced during our family sabbatical from August 2023 until April 2024. When you touch a tree 3,500 years old you realise the short timescales we run our home and work lives on. How compressed life is and how little time there is for us to slow down and to widen the aperture. Time seems different when you step away from day-to-day work and home life for a few months. You realize how much we rush, stress, overwhelm ourselves with too many commitments, projects at work and home. The result is exhausted kids, parents, employees and organizations. And exhausted minds are less able to do what they do best: focus and reflect.

The pressure to be busy, productive, outcome focussed, achieving KPIs, quarterly targets, hacks, time management techniques, cramming for exams leaves little time for stopping, pausing and reflecting.

In this article I explore not why we stop, pause and reflect but how and what implications this has for our professional lives and particularly how we design and deliver leadership programmes. When you are away and have more time it becomes clear that the modern world of work regards rest, downtime, or simply going for a walk at lunchtime as obstacles to be removed.

Stressed out Leaders

It is an assumption embedded in leadership programmes that time to step away and think is the main benefit of attending a programme. Yet why are timetables so packed? White space is often unconsciously perceived as 'dead time' by both the buyers and providers of leadership programmes. But how often as leadership coaches do we hear the opposite when working with leaders? I regularly hear comments such as *"I wish I had more time to just sit back, go for a walk, sit quietly on my own for an hour with no distraction, to be asked thoughtful questions I can mull over, to be liberated from the constant slew of work emails."* But these moments of insight and realization are snuffed out at the altar of productivity and busyness.

This sabbatical has afforded me lots of 'time to think', especially during all the hours of driving in our truck (vital as so many roads here in Argentina and Chile are unpaved). Visiting the Tambopata Research Centre deep in the Peruvian Amazon, for instance, I have seen the swathes of land cleared for agriculture and the gold-mining which pollutes the rivers.

Can any leadership programme be anything other than a climate, nature, and biodiversity programme? If the lifesystems we all depend on are not at the centre then what is?

When we stop, pause and reflect we widen the aperture. Our future cannot only be based on quarterly growth targets determined by external stakeholders. Patagonia founder Yvon Chouinard memorably

stated that the **Earth is now our only shareholder.** Yet despite all the talk of transformation, change, responsible business, ESG, regeneration when a coachee enters the room for their coaching session, which is often crowbarred into an already packed schedule, it seems that they are gasping for breath like deep sea divers who have been in the sea too long. They need to decompress.

All of us need more oxygen to breathe, to stop and to see what is going on around us, on our watch, negatively impacting our children and their future. But where is the energy in the midst of our own, personal energy crisis? Where is the mental space to see the larger system and its contribution to our crisis?

The pressure to be busy, productive, outcome focussed, achieving KPIs, quarterly targets, hacks, time management techniques, cramming for exams leaves little time for stopping, pausing and reflecting.

Breaktime

Taking the kids out of school, home schooling, turning down work, dealing with episodes of home sickness (we had to start watching the Grinch in October to get into the Christmas spirit!), bouts of sickness while couped up in a cabin no bigger than a chicken shed made us all think *why on earth did we do this*. But what opens up is time. Not always but more regularly. And high-quality time enables us to see experiences in different ways and which have the power to transform us and those around us. You also see the impact of beliefs and values that underpin not only the corporate world but also the world of education - kids are in a race and are either ahead or behind. Exams, pass or fail. But just consider what awaits our kids and how vital it will be for them to learn and apply reflective techniques essential to deal with 'wicked problems'.

Escape the city

Work and home life can often feel like a huge metropolis that never ends. To-dos multiply far off into the distance like a congested motorway. The city never sleeps. This perhaps explains why time in a natural place, whether that is our garden or on a glacier, revitalises our thinking. I felt this touching the 3,500 year old larch tree which surges upwards into the clear Patagonian sky. It needed space, light to stretch and grow. No wonder most of us feel over-whelmed. Even reflection can become yet another to-do that we never get round to because there is just, well, too much to do.

So why are so many leadership programmes packed with content like a dark, dense, regimented conifer plantation? Why is time to reflect and stop often seen as an add-on rather than integral to the purpose? Designing the content for a leadership programme is the easy bit. The tough bit is convincing a paying client that more time not doing anything pre-programmed is the most important part of a leadership programme.

The client is not always right

Now we will count to twelve
and we will all keep still
for once on the face of the earth,
let's not speak in any language;
let's stop for a second,
and not move our arms so much.

The client is not always right. Packing a leadership programme with content delivered by professors standing in lecture theatres is not reflection.

As experts in developing leaders our purpose is to enable busy, often distracted minds to cultivate the habit of reflection and to incorporate this into the day-to-day process of leadership.

So how can we incorporate more stopping, pausing and reflecting if we can agree that it is in the interstices that transformation might be found? We must try and turn an intangible into a value-creating activity.

But first let's count to twelve. This is a simple ritual I have adopted here in South America thanks to a poem by Chilean poet Pablo Neruda. As experts in developing leaders our purpose is to enable busy, often distracted minds to cultivate the habit of reflection and to incorporate this into the day-to-day process of leadership. But the habit rarely sticks. A New York lawyer I coached told me that he gets up at 04.30 am six days a week to answer emails from clients who all consider their case the most urgent. He runs to buy a sandwich and gobbles it down without chewing to save time. He would like to talk to his colleagues during his 10-minute lunch but does not have time. How is the system he is in adding or enhancing life systems?

It starts with counting to twelve with clients as well. When an HR Director briefs a provider about the needs of the business, we who provide learning and development services might encourage them to take twelve breaths. If we don't we get drawn into the whirlpool of busyness and sidestep the purpose of developing a leader in the first place - to put purpose, and by purpose I mean nature, climate and a regenerative economy ahead of profit. If not this then what, more profit? To achieve our own personal aims and ambitions? To change the direction of the business? To win? To launch new products and services?

Green thread

Leadership development surely can no longer be about our own purpose but the purpose of our times. And this calls for what I call a Green Thread running through all leadership programmes. The Red Thread, metrics, profit, KPIs etc, is easy and often needs little thinking. Leaders are likely to know this and feel comfortable when hearing a professor cover strategy or finance or technology. The Green Thread is different. It is possibly not front of mind for the HR or L&D Director. The Green Thread is the opposite of the Red Thread. The Green Thread binds each individual leader to a purpose that has a clear line of sight to all the circles.

The Green Thread is the opposite of the Red Thread. The Green Thread binds each individual leader to a purpose that has a clear line of sight to all the circles. In the centre of these concentric circles is nature and all that sustains our life on earth.

In the centre of these concentric circles is nature and all that sustains our life on earth.

We know a Red Thread without a Green Thread. Let me share a short example. I coached leaders attending a business school programme. The organisation ran Duty Free shops at airports. The CEO was clear that the one objective of the Programme was to teach the 30 leaders to better manage and grow their P&L. Neat. Simple. Measurable. And guaranteeing little learning. The Programme was packed. Coffee breaks, lunch were to be kept short so that minds could be filled with what the CEO deemed important. Attendees sat through hundreds of slides, over 50 models. They put together their Action Plans, left, and returned to their desks the same as when they had left. At no point was their thinking stretched and challenged.

Light and space are required for the larch tree to grow. The same for leaders.

The HR Director was happy as she had the metrics and feedback forms to show the CEO that his goal had been achieved. The Action Plans were forgotten as was the Programme. Coaching was easy as it was based on *have you or have you not increased profits six months after the programme.*

What lessons can be drawn out?

1. Coaching was a waste of time: my belief as a coach is that *tell me what you want to use the session for* leadership coaching is damaging. A leadership coach must enable the coachee to see what they did not see: the beliefs and values that constitute their mindset and the principles under which they act. Coaching is not about me but about us and is not about our own awareness but about awareness of our times and what is required in order to ensure life systems on earth continue to function and then flourish

2. The organization would continue as is. Business As Usual. The existing mindset and principles of the CEO and the culture would remain short-term, self-interest.

Pablo Neruda

3. A short-term, self-interest organization will fill a leadership programme with content and won't see the importance of the white as well as the black squares on a chessboard. Light and space are required for the larch tree to grow. The same for leaders.

As a freelance leadership coach I rely on a flow of work. If a nice juicy opportunity arises with a large bank I say 'yes' in two seconds which is why twelve seconds are needed. Then I can ask a very simple question prompted by the Neruda poem

Our role is to enable the leader to clear their own windscreen so they can see what is already there: systems breakdown. How we reflect is the starting point for any leadership programme.

If we were not so single-minded
about keeping our lives moving,
and for once could do nothing,
perhaps a huge silence
might interrupt this sadness
of never understanding ourselves
and of threatening ourselves with
Death.

What is the reason for this leadership programme? How do you want leaders to see things differently from how they currently see them? What would you like them to tell others about their experience when they return? What is the green thread running through the programme?

Power cut

We have had several since being here. You stop doing what you were doing and realize at that moment how driven we are by being constantly busy. But as Neruda says, the danger is that of *never understanding ourselves*. Leadership programmes should also be a version of a power cut. Yet most crowd out the white spaces on the chessboard with the black spaces. But why is it that participants will so often feedback that it was the moments outside the lecture theatre and away from the powerpoint slides that were the most meaningful? Pausing and stopping is a skill. It is a skill I believe to be the most valuable skill any leader can cultivate. It is a paradox then that attending a content-heavy leadership programme often stops the very process that is most needed: pausing, stopping and stepping back using a structure that is conducive to deeper critical thinking about our role as leaders in organizations and in the wider world.

One of the challenges is that we are still trapped by the illusion of knowledge. Effective leaders, so it goes, are those with the answers, the expert knowledge, the ability to fix and solve. This tame thinking is not reflection and is not the basis for a leadership programme.

Why is it that participants so often feedback that it was the moments outside the lecture theatre and away from the powerpoint slides that were the most meaningful? Pausing and stopping is a skill. It is a skill I believe to be the most valuable skill any leader can cultivate.

Ditch sustainability programmes

Good business, sustainability, ESG all appear in leadership conferences and programmes at some point, usually at the end! Yet, rather like coaching, all these words would be redundant if we reframed the process of leadership. Frameworks, reports, books, conferences are redundant when we ask a simple question - how do we each enhance life systems on earth? Not by increasing busyness. But by reducing it. And replacing it with chunks of time for reflection. Once you stop and look around you cannot unsee what is happening.

Our role is to enable the leader to clear their own windscreen so they can see what is already there: systems breakdown. How we reflect is the starting point for any leadership programme. This is the green thread that must run through all leadership programmes.

Mark McCartney is a leadership coach and facilitator. He enables leaders across the world to thrive in our rapidly changing world. He has a specialism in helping working dads in senior positions to find satisfaction at work and home and to start thinking about their legacy for their children and generations to come who want to live on a healthy planet. https://www.linkedin.com/in/markmccartneythedadcoach

By Roddy Millar

Lessons from the Maasai

3Rs – Responsibility, Ritual and Rulers

What is it that makes organizations operate smoothly and efficiently? Why do some seem to fly to the moon while others crash to earth? Why is the average age of large organizations falling? There are, of course, no simple answers to these questions – if there were they wouldn't be worth asking, and we would all understand the dynamics well.

These conundrums persist as they are complex, with a palimpsest of factors layering on top of each other. We have a natural tendency to seek hard numbers to explain problems, they are so much easier to work with

– and manipulate - but they can rarely provide the whole picture. For me, as editor of a magazine focused on leadership, the underlying reason is founded on the fuzzy human factors.

Often when we are presented with complexity the best thing to do is to step-back and try and visualize the main elements as a simpler model, and once we have a good understanding of that, then dial-up the complexity to see where the issues can be resolved or at least relieved.

It was with this approach that I spent a week with the Maasai in Kenya, in the company of Anthony Willoughby, who has a long association and close friendship with those we were staying with, and a group of interested others, ranging in age from 14 to mid-70s.

The Maasai are the iconic tribe of East Africa. They are nomadic pastoralists – that is traditionally they moved with their herds of cattle, sheep and goats on a continual circuit to fresh pasturelands. In recent decades the Kenyan government has applied stricter land regulation across the country, meaning that there is less freedom for nomadic herders to roam. This has forced the Maasai to become more static in their ways, leading to them living in more permanently settled communities, and inevitably this has brought change to their traditional way of life.

In recent decades the Kenyan government has applied stricter land regulation across the country, meaning that there is less freedom for nomadic herders to roam.

Alongside this change, the modern world has equally inevitably impinged on their lives. From actively having sought to remain separate from modernizing influences, and so government structures, today they realize that to have any influence over their domains they need to be part of the conversation. They are gradually, though in many cases reluctantly, becoming advocates of western-styled education which those we stayed with stressed, teaches knowledge but not wisdom, which the Maasai value more than knowledge. Children will walk long distances at a young age to go to school – and a significant number aspire to go on to college and university. These changes bring greater interaction with the modern world and create tensions between traditional ways of life and new ones. For instance, as Kenya has led the way in mobile technology, and the opportunities it can bring – principally through M-Pesa, the mobile banking service – the outside world and commerce is no more than a click away.

The challenge for nomadic peoples, like the Maasai, is how they can find a path to balance these tensions. Can they maintain a cohesive and collaborative community while the attractions of the modern world lure their young to the cities?

The challenge for nomadic peoples, like the Maasai, is how they can find a path to balance these tensions. Can they maintain a cohesive and collaborative community while the attractions of the modern world lure their young to the cities? This question is not so dissimilar from that which executives are asking themselves and their boards, about their employees – how do we create a loyalty, a sense of belonging amongst our staff that will make them want to stay? There will always be greener grass elsewhere, so what can be done to make organizations more attractive to stay with?

I first spent time with a group of Maasai in 2019 and was struck by their extraordinary sense of community. Like so many traditional societies they have practices and traditions that have impacts that may at first not be apparent – but the elders amongst them are deeply aware of the importance of these practices.

It is worth noting, that while this article seeks to highlight some of the practices that we in the more economically developed west could valuably adopt – or readopt, as they are mainly practices we have abandoned and forgotten – the Maasai way is not an ideal, there are many things people in the west (and increasingly the Maasai too) would not wish to embrace which are neither beneficial nor benevolent. Foremost is that it is a patriarchal society, women certainly have influence, but very much less so than men; and the structure of the groups is such that it promotes cohesion over change, so innovation can be slow to occur. Emmanuel Mankura who leads one of the communities we were staying with is doing all he can to break many of these barriers and taboos in his community – including FGM.

The moving parts of a nomadic herds-people's lives may be less complex than those in a fast-moving modern city, but nonetheless, no life is simple especially with the onslaught of climate change; many communities have seen up to 90% of their cattle die in the recent drought. And where there are people, there are complications as well as solutions. That relative simplicity, however, provides an opportunity to see the moving parts more clearly.

Responsibility, Ritual and Rules

Responsibility

Lolkerra may only be five years old, and his mother still have to cook for him and wash his clothes, but regardless of this he has been given a responsibility that he primarily enjoys, but also that he takes very seriously. Lolkerra is tasked with taking a goat out to pasture, and more importantly, bringing it back at the end of each day. He does not do this entirely alone, there is a group of young Maasai children who have their own animals – and they do not go far from the manyatta, or homestead of three huts. Rarely even out of sight of it. But nonetheless, the goat is Lolkerra's responsibility to look after – and live-stock are the central wealth of the Maasai.

When he is older he will become a warrior and look after the cattle. These may need to be taken away from the manyatta for days or even weeks in search of fresh grazing, depending on the season and the rains – but the path towards doing that starts at a very young age.

The giving of responsibility to people is a fundamental element of creating purpose in our lives. Ultimately, we all want to 'matter', we want to matter to other people, whether colleagues, friends or family and we want our work to matter. If what we do matters to no-one, or is so replicable that no-one cares who does it, we disengage. You don't care, so I don't care.

In the Maasai, the tending of livestock lies at the very heart of their existence. It is centrally important – it is their wealth, their key to trading for other goods they do not have, and the source of their sustenance too. Livestock matters – so being given responsibility for a

goat matters too. And with that understanding comes an awareness that they have a place in the community. It may not be pivotal, but it is an essential part of the successful functioning of the community.

We spend an enormous amount of time and resource selecting, interviewing and then on-boarding new people into our organizations – and all too often we then fail to give them responsibility for anything meaningful. Decisions are all shifted up the hierarchy or to committees, slowing progress and over-burdening leaders, while leaving able and eager new employees feeling disengaged, and wondering if the work they do 'matters'. Perhaps we should all look around and see if there is a metaphorical goat we can entrust to people, where they can have more decision-making power and responsibility that matters.

The moving parts of a nomadic herdspeople's lives may be less complex than those in a fast-moving modern city, but nonetheless, no life is simple especially with the onslaught of climate change.

Ritual

One of the most striking and beguiling parts of spending any time with the Maasai is their enthusiasm to sing, dance and engage in traditional ritual. The group we spent time with were well off the tourist trail, and there was a real sense of excitement and fiesta when our party arrived at their village – having walked there from our camp through the bush, guided by some young 'warriors' and elders.

At the village gates we were greeted by all the women-folk singing a song of welcome. It was a surprisingly emotional experience. It is well understood that collective singing is a hugely bonding experience[1] – it being both an expression of unity as well as an activity that brings people together. While communal singing is not prevalent in organizations, though the likes of *Music*

---

1   Medial Conditions for Social Bonding in Singing https://www.jstor.org/stable/48640868

The lack of a single 'figurehead' chief is important. It creates a radically different mindset within the collective, be that a tribe or an organization. Power does not coalesce around a single individual.

in Offices in London are leveraging this power effectively, there are plenty of community choirs in the west which draw people in and create a sense of belonging and community. Perhaps what is less normal in western groups is male dance groups. The Maasai are well-known for their unique dance style, *adumu*. This is where the young warriors dance competitively by jumping up and down on the spot, rhythmically to the singing of their peers. The performance is a combination of prowess, strength and unbridled joy and laughter, all with the background swell of the primal rhythmic singing.

It is difficult to immediately see where a parallel or similar activity can be brought into work organizations. In smaller organizations and often within teams or groups there are 'offsites' and 'away days', but they don't usually hold any 'ritual' sense to them. The closest to that perhaps is the Christmas Party, but the rituals there are often ones that do less to bond people in, than people seek to avoid! The lack of office ritual has become more apparent since the pandemic and the rise of working-from-home. Sport tends to be better at building rituals into their practices, the pre-match routines and post-match celebrations or consolations.[2]

What is clear with the Maasai though, is that these communal rituals – and they extend far beyond singing and dancing, to the rites of passage for boys as they become 'warriors' and the bleeding of cattle for blood, or the 'meat camps' that the men sometimes go on, all weave a sense of belonging and pride into their Maasai-ness. Other parts of the route to maturity are having to change though - the identity that came from the courage required for killing a lion no longer exists, lion-killing now being outlawed, thus the community we were in is 'teaching' that the pen is their new spear and the sheet of paper is their new shield. "An educated man never goes hungry" being the new mantra.

By participating you feel part of the group – and as you get older, that moment of participation looms ahead of you, drawing you inwards and onwards in the group, until you are part of it. It not only acts as an incentive to keep going, but there is also a sense that if you leave the group you lose that connection and ability to participate in something that your peers all really value. Rituals really become glue for the group.

---

2   McKinsey on Rituals https://www.mckinsey.com/capabilities/people-and-organizational-performance/our-insights/workplace-rituals-recapturing-the-power-of-what-weve-lost

Good leaders need to identify the activities that can act as, or be evolved into, workplace rituals. They should be joyful and seen by all, though the ability to take part may only come as certain milestones are achieved. They should not be confused with perks though. The car park space or additional holidays are not rituals.

Rulers

Perhaps the most significant lesson we can learn from the Maasai – and many other indigenous groups too – is that they are run by a network of elders, with no single chief. It is a very human model that has been practiced by *homo sapiens* for millennia. Leadership and responsibility are shared amongst a group of elders. When challenges arise the most experienced elder in that area is consulted, or a group of elders discuss the issue.

For major challenges the discussion is opened to a wider audience and a collective decision is taken, which everyone must adhere to. Clearly this is a simpler process when you are managing a group of 30-150 people than an organization of thousands. Above 150 and collective decision-making becomes chaotic usually. However, the need for large group decisions is rare, both in tribes and in commercial organizations.

The lack of a single 'figurehead' chief is important though. It creates a radically different mindset within the collective, be that a tribe or an organization. Power does not coalesce around a single individual, there will inevitably be some senior elders who are 'more equal than others', that have more influence and informal authority. But by keeping the field of senior elders broad it allows everyone to feel that they have a pathway to influencing the tribe if they wish. Anthony Willoughby recalls asking a group of Maasai elders 'who is the leader here?' and they simply replied "Everyone is a leader, please can you tell us the problem you wish to solve and we will select the most appropriate person to solve it." In today's business world, no single person has all the answers, so a move to more distributed leadership has been occurring for some time, but hierarchies still tend to culminate in single individuals.

It should be noted that while senior elders certainly are deeply respected, they are not necessarily any wealthier or better provided for. The route to senior elderhood is essentially one of community acclaim. The more respected you are for your behaviour – and maybe your prowess at various activities be that hunting or medicine or conflict management or some other valuable skill - the more valued your opinion and greater your influence on discussion.

This sets a tone and a pathway in indigenous groups that is very different to that of the modern

commercial or bureaucratic organization. An individual's pathway to a position of influence emerges out of how they are viewed by the rest of the group. Without concrete positions for people to aim for and obtain, there is less politicking to be done to secure such roles. Marshall Goldsmith's 2008 book, *What Got You Here Wont Get You There*, describes the often practiced dog-eat-dog tactics of the climb up the corporate ladder which are not what makes a good CEO who really needs to be 'in service to the whole organization' and not just 'in service to themselves'. In order to progress to positions of influence and respect you

have to be 'in service to the whole organization' from the very beginning. Any indication of being 'in service to yourself' is a quick route to losing influence. When Willoughby once asked Joseph Nombri, a worldly Papua New Guinean elder, 'how do you select leaders?' his reply was "We watch who people follow."

There is an interesting circularity here – as Lolk-erra with his goat learned from an early age that to gain respect from his parents and those close around him, he needed to look after the goat attentively – the sense of being 'in service to the organization' also began at that point.

Elders as a collective group, do not have a need to be 'commanding', their approach is much more observational and accessible. They are happy for others, the more active and energetic young (though you can be a senior elder from a relatively early age – in your mid-30s even) to make their impact and create progress for the tribe.

This can cut both ways, it does mean that for much of the time the tribe/organization is not being encouraged to surge forward, grow and dominate. That works well for a tribe and society, it is more risky for many capitalist organizations where attack is often the only form of defence.

Elders do not have a need to be 'commanding', their approach is much more to be observational and accessible

Leadership

From a leadership perspective, where the leaders are creating the conditions for others to do their best work in pursuit of a common objective, this Maasai/indigenous peoples' approach is very effective. By building responsibility and so a sense of purpose; binding members into the group through practices and rituals that fosters their sense of self and belonging; and managing the collective with a looser, broader group of guides as elders, a sustainably cohesive and mutually cooperative organization develops.

As mentioned earlier, the Maasai way is far from a panacea or ideal, but there are lessons to be learnt and absorbed, on how with a different, more collective, mindset the human side of the group gains, to use the modern term, greater psychological safety, and a more cohesive, harmonious and happier and sustainable way of operating ensues.

By Wendy Shepherd

Leadership Program ROI

Useful Fact or Mythical Fiction?

Why we should abandon ROI as the Holy Grail in Leadership Development Impact Measurement

I recently read a paper that described return on investment (ROI) as a measure of Leadership Development Impact as the Holy Grail. It sat atop a pyramid that consisted of five levels, the first four of which were taken from Kirkpatrick's model of Training Validation.

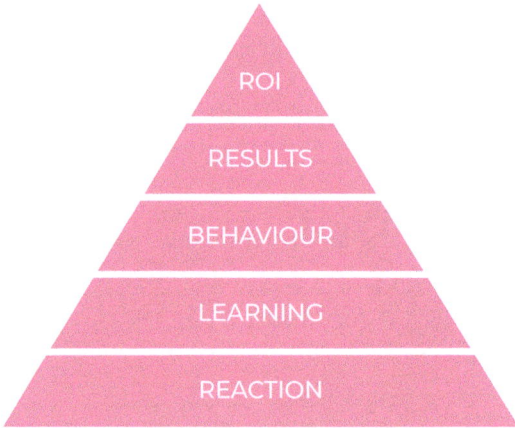

Fig one: The Value Pyramid

The paper went on to make suggestions as to how this illusive figure could be calculated.

The Holy Grail is a mythical object first featuring in a medieval novel by Chretien de Troyes. I would argue that the calculation of ROI from leadership development is on occasion (if not always) also a great work of fiction.

The problem starts with the misconception that *objective* measures should take precedence over *subjective* measures. If executive development can even loosely be linked to an objective measure, that measure is often assumed to be more reliable than the firsthand account of benefits provided by those who attended the development.

The second problem is that the Kirkpatrick Model with Phillips ROI grafted on at the top is often interpreted as a value chain that goes something like this:

| REACTION | LEARNING | BEHAVIOUR | RESULTS | ROI |

Figure Two: The Impact Chain

If we examine each of these links in the impact chain, we reveal challenges that make the model and any calculation of ROI unsound:

Assumption 1 – A positive reaction to development is the first stage in the impact chain

Without doubt we don't want those who attend executive development to have a torrid time. There is no greater pleasure than collecting in happy sheets that describe the development as favourable, engaging and relevant.

But are high satisfaction scores really the first step in a chain of impactful development?

Initially produced to explain reactions to grief and loss, and more recently employed to explain the range of emotions associated with organizational change, the Kubler-Ross Change Curve suggests that meaningful change can occur from initial feelings of shock, denial, anger, frustration, and uncertainty.

Negative emotions during or immediately after a development process may occur where aspects of the development conflict with specific participants' world view. These participants may eventually gain more from their development than those who find it agreeable and give it little extra thought.

The problem starts with the misconception that objective measures should take precedence over subjective measures.

Assumption 2 – For impact to occur their must first be learning

Learning is one source of development impact. It is however, not the only one. Equally beneficial are the relationships formed, the conversations had, the feelings of self-worth generated by investment and the chance to step back from the day to day and reflect on what is happening and what might lie ahead.

When applied to Leadership Development, the Kirkpatrick model encourages an over simplified perspective of leadership, as a universally relevant set of actions and capabilities that can be improved through training; rather than a more contemporary perspective of leadership as a socially complex, situationally emergent phenomenon that is not trainable.

What good leadership development does is stimulate the participants to generate new reflections on their own experiences, broaden their thought/action repertoires and alter commitment to different courses of action. The value of learning is therefore not so much in how to use models and frameworks, but what is discovered through their application i.e. the train of thought or discussion that emerges and where it leads.

Meaningful change can occur from initial feelings of shock, denial, anger, frustration, and uncertainty.

Assumption 3: When learning is applied it has an impact on the leader's behaviour

The assumption that learning is evidenced through changes in behaviour is a hangover from the temptation to oversimplify leadership to a trainable quality. There may well be changes in behaviour that can be immediately witnessed following leadership development, and there may be value associated with these changes. But there may also be value in things that are not observable, for example, how do you observe a change in a course of action that would have been taken but has not due to the application of learning? How do you isolate changes in behaviour associated with other environmental factors to only identify changes that have been initiated by the development?

Often when it comes to measuring behaviours, we reach for a 360° tool which we see as objective, but the 360 is based on the opinion of others and the attribution of their personal values and sense of what good looks like. It therefore lacks the objectivity that the presence of a Likert scale may suggest.

Assumption 4: Results

At stage four we look for tangible results that we can link to development. Suggestions have been made that metrics associated with Employee Engagement, Staff Retention and Client Satisfaction are all potentially viable. The greatest flaw in the desire to link organizational metrics to leadership development is that there is no proof of causality and the impact of development cannot be isolated from other factors that have an impact on the measures. This can lead to overclaims of impact where measures have improved and explaining away the relevance when things take a turn for the worse.

Assumption 5: ROI

Putting a financial figure on the improvements witnessed is the last link in a chain of flawed assumptions about leadership development and the impact it has. Those who seek to put a financial figure on development often do so by monetizing the results witnessed at Step 4.

The problem here is that the value generated by a change in these metrics is almost never down to the actions of one leader, furthermore, the actions of a leader are not going to be entirely due to what they have learnt during development. This assumption presupposes that they knew nothing prior to the development intervention.

Calculating ROI can be expensive because of the amount of data that has to be collected. Even when there is a figure, and even if the figure were a close representation of the benefits, the results cannot be assumed to be 'fixed' benefits that will be achieved every time the development is run.

The nature of leadership development is that the benefits are emergent, variable according to the changing context of the organization and the makeup of the participants and what they carry into the room.

Conclusion

If we are to move ahead with our understanding of the impact of leadership development, we need to be brave and walk away from long held assumptions that proliferate from the use of models such as Kirkpatrick and Philips ROI. This requires us to develop new models of evaluation associated with the contemporary requirements of leadership within specific contexts.

When it comes to leadership development nothing will work in all contexts for all participants. A positive impact from Leadership Development starts with a clarity of purpose linked to the specific participants' context. This can inform the design; help manage the progress of participants; and finally, be used for evaluation. The impact chain recommended by Kirkpatrick and

Philips is reactive, beginning once development has been completed, the money has been spent and the opportunity has been lost. The impact chain being suggested here is more proactive, not only addressing proof of impact but also the design and management of impact.

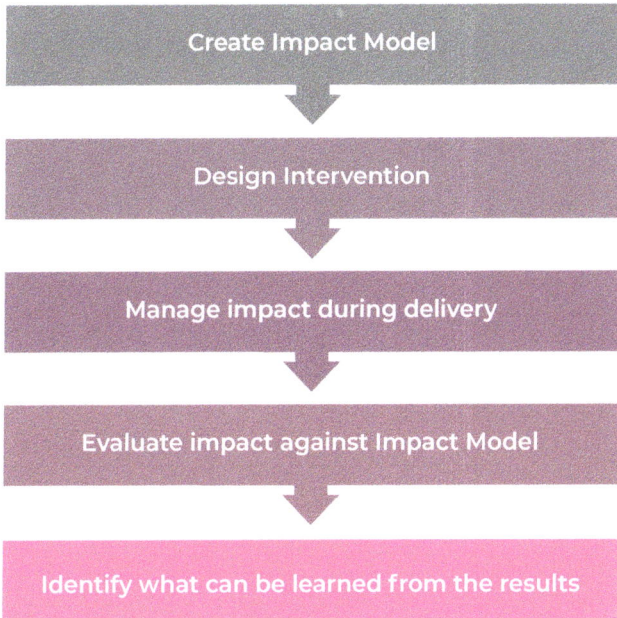

Figure Three: A Proactive Impact Chain

If the design of an intervention starts with the creation of an impact model that defines expectations

In the longer term it may be possible to attach a financial value to the outcome of these changes, but this should not be the primary goal.

of where and how change will occur, it will be possible to track progress and steer development towards these context specific aims. Furthermore, if aims are defined and progress tracked using a consistent categorization of expectations across leadership development designs, it will be possible, over time, to develop and share new insights, such as how online development impacts the opportunity for building networks and relationships.

The table that follows suggests a new categorization of outcomes. This is based on recent research, including a review of leadership development case studies and interviews with practitioners. Five categories have been identified but there may be more.

The categories recommended represent initial changes in leadership activity rather than long term outcomes. Changes in these categories can be identified by questionnaire within three months of participants completing their development. It therefore has the potential to be a cost-effective solution to the challenge of evaluation.

As the evaluation takes place within a short period of time and focuses on what the participants have done as a consequence of their development, we can be confident of a causal link. In the longer term it may be possible to attach a financial value to the outcome of these changes, but this should not be the primary goal. The aim should be to identify grassroot changes in leadership activity associated with a specific development design and context, so that we might learn what has worked, and perhaps more importantly not worked so well.

CATEGORY ONE: COMMUNICATIONS	Developed through facilitated discussions, the application of theory to the organizational context, the socialization of participants and the input of senior sponsors. Changes in conversation during and after the development generate knowledge sharing; learning; coordination; and followership. Many participants go on to share what they have learnt within the development setting with their teams or facilitate new discussions about the topics discussed. This brings more people into discussions across the organization.
CATEGORY TWO: SENSEMAKING	Developed through active reflection, witnessing a breadth of perspectives and the application of theory. Changes in sensemaking generate problem setting and solving; initiate new or amended actions; and changes in tolerance; empathy; and commitment.
CATEGORY THREE: RELATIONSHIPS AND NETWORKS	Developed through the socialization of participants across the cohort and with senior sponsors. This may create a sense of community; build trust and followership; and increase the organizational visibility of individuals. The benefit to relationships may not just be interpersonal, but also break down silos between functions, units or geographies. Changes in relationships and networks can generate access to resources; and increase collaboration, learning, efficiency and innovation.

CATEGORY FOUR: ALIGNMENT OF BEHAVIOURS AND PRIORITIES	Developed through group discussion; direction; the leadership of participants and sponsors; the application of common frameworks; and mimicry. The alignment of behaviours and priorities has implications for the corporate culture and brand, potentially generating synergies and alliances for change.
CATEGORY FIVE: ENGAGEMENT	Developed as a consequence of being invested in, being inspired by tutors, other participants or programme sponsors. Beyond the intervention, changes in the way the participants interact with their teams may also lead to further changes in levels of engagement amongst the wider organizational population. Changes in levels of engagement affect discretionary effort; wellbeing; productivity; and the retention of employees.

The approach presented in this article has been field tested at Cranfield School of Management using a toolkit to support each stage of the value chain. For more information please contact me at Cranfield School of Management or via www.linkedin.com/in/dr-wendy-shepherd-cranfield.

*Winner of the 2021 AMBA and BGA award for the impact of her doctoral thesis. **Wendy Shepherd** is an expert in learning design and Impact with responsibility for the design and Impact of executive development programmes delivered by Cranfield School of Management.* **https://www.linkedin.com/in/dr-wendy-shepherd-cranfield/**

IDEAS FOR LEADERS

Academic research in
accessible and engaging
bite-sized chunks

WHY FOLLOWERS MAKE GREAT LEADERS

KEY CONCEPT

People who identify as leaders are perceived as leaders by their superiors. Peers, however, are more likely to see leadership qualities in those among them who identify as followers—because these individuals are more inclined to put the goals of the group above their own goals.

IDEA SUMMARY

One of the dominant assumptions in leadership theory is that some people are meant to lead and others are meant to follow. This assumption is based on the belief that the mindset and behaviours of a leader—to want to take charge, to be dominant, confident, and optimistic—are completely different from the mindset and behaviours of a follower, who will be industrious, good citizens of the group and happy to let others take the lead.

This mutually exclusive assumption of leadership and followership also leads to the conclusion that people who see themselves as leaders are more likely to be seen as leaders by others, while people who see themselves as followers are more likely to be perceived as followers.

Studies have indeed shown that self-identity can play a role in one's leadership development—that is, individuals who see themselves as leaders are more likely to emerge as leaders. However, there is little evidence, some social scientists argue, that individuals who see themselves as followers cannot emerge as leaders. One study shows, for example, that individuals can have both leadership and followership traits within them. Another study indicates that people looking for leaders will turn to those who have shown followership.

Two researchers from the University of Queensland, Prof. Kim Peters and Prof. S. Alexander Haslam, decided to test the link between self-identity, as either a leader or a follower, and eventual perceptions of leadership qualities. Peters and Haslam predicted that while those who identified as leaders could be perceived as leaders by others, those who identified as followers could also be perceived as leaders.

This second assertion was based on their belief that a followership identity would motivate individuals to put the needs and goals of the group above their own needs and goals—which, according to social identity theory, would elevate their influence in the group.

The context of the research was a 32-week training course for a group of 218 Royal Marine recruits. (Because of the rigorous course's high attrition rate, the eventual sample would total 68 recruits.) The study measured:

- **Recruit self-identity**. The Royal Marines recruits were surveyed five times during the course on whether they identified as leaders or followers. The surveys used a 7-point Likert scale (from 1 strongly disagree to 7 strongly agree) for statements such as "I think I am a natural leader" or "I think it is more important to get the job done than to get my way".
- **Commander evaluation of recruits**. The troop commanders were surveyed on their recruits' leadership and followership —through similar statements and a Likert scale for responses—midway through the training and at the end.
- **Recruit evaluation of their peers**. Finally, at the end

of the training, the recruits evaluated their peers' leadership through the vote for the Commando Medal; this vote requires recruits to rate each member of their group on whether they embody the "commando spirit".

The results of the study showed that:
1. Commanders were more likely to perceive as leaders recruits who identified as leaders and perceive as followers recruits who identified as followers.
2. Recruits selected as leaders individuals in their troops who identified as leaders and individuals who identified as followers.

These results confirm that identifying as a follower does not eliminate the potential for being perceived as a leader by others, but with a nuance: Who those others might be makes a difference. The difference depends on whether one's perspective is external (as in the troop commanders) or internal (as in the peers of the recruits). External observers are less likely to perceive leadership qualities in individuals who identify as followers.

Three reasons can explain this difference. The first is that superiors do not witness those actions by followers that reveal their commitment to the group and thus increase their influence. Second, superiors will notice individuals who identify as leaders since these individuals will deliberately seek to display their leadership abilities to them. Finally, superiors and group members may have different viewpoints on leadership. In this case, the recruits may be focused on the training context in which commitment to the group is paramount. The commanders may be looking for signs of broader leadership qualities required for a successful military career.

BUSINESS APPLICATION

Whatever the underlying reasons, the perception differences between superiors and peers revealed by the study hold an important lesson for managers and leaders in organizations looking to develop potential leaders: the importance of recognizing that in some ways, superiors are outsiders who may not witness leadership behaviours that occur within the group. Because the ability to influence others is at the heart of leadership, the perception of an individual's peers is one of the most revealing indications of future leadership potential. Incorporating peer evaluations is thus key to effective leadership assessment and leadership development processes.

REFERENCES
I follow, therefore I lead: A longitudinal study of leader and follower identity and leadership in the marines. Kim Peters and S. Alexander Haslam. British Journal of Psychology (November 2018). https://bpspsychub.onlinelibrary.wiley.com/doi/abs/10.1111/bjop.12312

Access this and more Ideas at ideasforleaders.com

IDEA #854

FOLLOWERS CAN FIX THE DAMAGE OF LEADERSHIP INCOMPETENCE

KEY CONCEPT

Restorative behavior by followers can restore damaged relationships and lost value caused by leadership incompetence.

IDEA SUMMARY

Leadership involves a dynamic relationship between leader and follower to which both parties contribute. The study of "followership," focuses on the vital role that followers play in the leader-follower relationship and, consequently, the role that followers play in the success of the organization. For example, poor followership, such as blindly following an incompetent or unethical leader, can be as damaging to an organization as poor leadership.

Two scholars of African leadership and followership offer a unique perspective on the role of followership when dealing with "bad" leaders a perspective based on the concept of restorative behavior.

Restorative behavior refers to the actions and reactions of followers attempting to restore relationships whose values have been damaged by the negative actions of their leaders. Effective relationships between an organizational leader and his or her followers lead to value creation for the organization; this value is lost when the relationship is undermined by the leader.

The research of Baniyelme Zoogah of Xavier University's Williams College of Business and James Abugre of the University of Ghana Business School focused on poor leadership in terms of incompetence, defined as the inability to influence followers through effective communication and engagement. Specifically, incompetent leaders fail to involve followers in decision-making, fail to communicate with transparency and fail to ask for information or to act on information and suggestions offered by followers.

Through a series of surveys conducted with groups and dyads of supervisors and followers, Zoogah and Abugre found that:

- Incompetent leadership induced followers to undertake restorative behaviors to undo the harm of the incompetence restorative behaviors included discerning the causes and outcomes of the leader's incompetence; a willingness to hold the leader accountable; a willingness to express concerns to the leader; and, finally, taking actions to restore the value of the relationship, including offering potential solutions to improve communication and participative decision-making.

- Whether followers enacted restorative behaviors was linked to some extent to whether the followers were actively engaged that is, whether they cared about and were invested in the relationship with their leaders and the value that emanated from those relationships. The research suggested that leader incompetence would push followers to become more actively engaged.

• At the same time, the research showed that follower-leader value fit that is, how closely the values of the leaders were aligned with the values of the followers acted as a substitute for active engagement in spurring followers to action. In other words, when the leader-follower value fit was high, active engagement was less important in prompting followers to take action. However, when the leader-follower fit was low, high active engagement was key to followers taking the initiative to engage in restorative behaviors.

• Finally, in general, the research shows that restorative behavior led to restorative value in other words, the value created out of the relationship between the leaders and followers could be restored. To the surprise of the researchers, however, discernment, accountability, and voice did not have the same impact on restorative value as restorative repair.

BUSINESS APPLICATION

This research was based in Africa, which at the national level has a history of restorative behaviour in response to leadership incompetence or malfeasance. The Truth and Reconciliation Commission of South Africa may be the most famous example of the application of restorative behaviour, but it is not the only one.

This research reveals the effectiveness of restorative behaviour at the organisational level and implies certain steps organisations can take to encourage restorative behaviour by followers, including:

- Giving followers the psychological safety to engage in restorative behaviour.
- Ensuring that there is a value fit between leaders and their followers.
- Encouraging a community of healing by helping leaders and followers to interact when leadership behaviour has damaged their relationships. This community of healing should be based on a "respect for all" culture that focuses on harms and needs, addresses obligations, and promotes collaboration and inclusiveness.
- Inducing the active engagement of followers with systems and processes that enable this engagement.

REFERENCES
Restorative followership in Africa: Antecedents, moderators, and consequences. Baniyelme D. Zoogah and James B. Abugre. Africa Journal of Management (July 2020). https://www.tandfon-line.com/doi/full/10.1080/23322373.2020.1777818

Access this and more Ideas at ideasforleaders.com

GENDER DIVERSE TEAMS ARE MORE INNOVATIVE AND IMPACTFUL

KEY CONCEPT

Gender-diverse teams produce more innovative and impactful research, according to an in-depth study of 20 years of medical sciences research papers. The rigorous requirements for quality in this field implies that gender diversity would have an equally beneficial impact on the quality of team performance in other fields.

IDEA SUMMARY

An analysis of 6.6 million papers related to the medical sciences published between 2000 and 2021 showed that the proportion of gender-diverse teams involved in medical research is growing steadily for all team sizes. The gender diversity of research teams of four members, for example, increased by 10% in that period (from 60% in 2000 to 70% in 2019).

The study shows, however, that there is still room for progress. The number of gender-diverse teams publishing research was underrepresented in all team sizes, in some cases by as much as 17%, according to the analysis. That is, the researchers' statistical modelling showed that depending on the team size, up to nearly 1/5th of the same-gender teams would have been gender-mixed had team members been assigned without attention to gender.

The study's insight into the quality of the research from mixed gender teams is particularly interesting. According to the analysis, the research published by mixed-gender teams was more novel and impactful than the research published by same-gender teams of the same size. The novelty measure, which indicates how much a paper combines past knowledge in new ways, was based on atypical combination of references. That is, if two references not normally seen in the same paper were used, the paper was deemed more novel than a paper in which its references are often seen together. The impact measure, which indicates how much a paper influences future work, was based on how many times the paper was cited by other researchers. Specifically, papers who reached the top 5% of citations in a given year were considered impactful.

The study also established a link between gender balance and quality. The greater the gender balance—the more closely the teams were evenly distributed between men and women members—the more novel and impactful the research. The researchers recognized that other factors might explain the success, in terms of novelty and impact, of gender-diverse team publications. Analysing the professional and personal background and demographics of the authors, the researchers found that mixed-gender teams had greater diversity in expertise, career stage, and geographic background—which could explain, but only partly, the high level of novelty and impact of gender-diverse teams' research.

BUSINESS APPLICATION

Using medical scientific papers for the context of their study, the researchers' in-depth analysis of the 6.6 million papers' authors supports the contention that gender diversity adds to a team's innovativeness and performance. The study further shows the importance of gender balance, indicating that token diversity is not only cynical but also often unproductive.

Although it is focused on one professional domain, given the hard, objective requirements of research in this domain, the implications of these results can be applied to organizations and companies in other fields—as in product development, for example.

The authors of this study do not intend to overstate the role of gender diversity in team performance. Indeed, they explored the influence of other factors, such as diversity of expertise and career stage, that could have contributed to the novelty and impact of the research in question. It is possible and plausible, however, that gender diversity could have led to the diversity of expertise and career stage and even geographic background on many of these teams. And it cannot be ignored that the key term in all of these factors is diversity. Creating homogeneous teams, it can be argued, increases the chances of less-optimal performance.

REFERENCES
Restorative followership in Africa: Antecedents, moderators, and consequences. Baniyelme D. Zoogah and James B. Abugre. Africa Journal of Management (July 2020). https://www.tandfonline.com/doi/full/10.1080/23322373.2020.1777818

Access this and more Ideas at **ideasforleaders.com**

LEADERS' MANAGEMENT OF TEAM EMOTIONS KEY TO AGILE SUCCESS

KEY CONCEPT

While agile management may feature innovative tools and processes, how well team leaders manage emotions in agile teams can make the difference between high agility and low agility—and the ultimate success of the team in responding to crises and change.

IDEA SUMMARY

The agile management approach, which began as a project management approach in the field of software product development, rejects rigid structures and processes in favour of customer-focused incremental processes that respond and adapt continuously to changing developments and customer feedback. Numerous methodologies have been developed to ensure the flexibility and responsiveness at the heart of this approach.

These methodologies, as well as academic research on Agile management, focus heavily on team structures, tools, and processes (e.g., self-organized teams, daily stand-up meetings, Kanban boards, etc.) In contrast, a study of teams of nurses in the Middle East facing a series of crises reveal a factor essentially ignored by agile practitioners, consultants, and researchers: the role of emotions in the success or failure of agile teams.

Prof. Murat Tarakci of the Rotterdam School of Management and Max-Antoine Renault, a researcher at Sidra Medicine research hospital in Doha, Qatar, conducted a two-year study of pediatric nursing teams navigating three crises sequentially: sudden floods, organizational upheavals that significantly affected the nurses' working and living conditions, and the Covid-19 pandemic. Although all the teams used agile methodologies, the researchers asked ward managers responsible for several clinics in the hospital to assess the speed, responsiveness, and flexibility their nursing teams. These assessments allowed the researchers to differentiate high-agility teams from low-agility teams. They eventually settled on nine nursing teams, five high-agility and four low-agility, for their study.

During the two-year study period, the researchers conducted 45 interviews with ward managers, team leaders, and nurses, attended 19 daily huddles, surveyed nurses on their emotions following or during each of the three crises described above, and during the Covid 19 pandemic, monitored more than 1,000 WhatsApp messages sent by nurses in two of the teams.

The research revealed the high emotions that ran in the teams because of the crises. The Covid-19 pandemic, for example, engendered feelings of fear, distress, and nervousness, according to the research surveys. Yet, in the high-agility teams, nurses also shared their emotions of pride, strength, and inspiration in dealing with the crisis. As evidence by observations of team huddles and WhatsApp messages, these individual positive emotions translated into a more positive team environment in high-agility teams compared to the negative team environments in low-agility teams.

The difference, according to the researchers, can be explained by the consistent effort of team leaders in high-agile teams to recalibrate team members' negative emotions—that is, to navigate the team away from negative emotions toward more positive emotions.

To achieve this recalibration, which was missing in low-agile teams, high-agile team leaders recognized and accepted that individual emotions in crisis situations would vary; believed that tending to the team's emotional needs was part of their mandate as leader; and made a special effort to thank and praise team members. Critically, the high-agile team leaders also proactively discouraged the formation of cliques. In times of distress, individuals tend to gather in small groups to offer support to each other. While low-agile team leaders did not see the harm in such cliques, high-agile team leaders recognized that the isolation of team members outside the cliques, or the presence of several cliques, would contribute to a lack of unity and unified support in the team.

Indeed, the researchers found that by managing team emotions, including helping individuals through their unique emotional responses, and preventing cliques, high-agile leaders strengthened the unity and team-work of their teams—which in turn allowed these teams, according to the research, to respond with more agility and more successfully to the crises they confronted.

BUSINESS APPLICATION

This research has clear managerial implications.

- **Actively and proactively monitor and manage the emotional well-being of agile teams**. Different team members react differently to change—e.g., some will be distressed, while others inspired by the possibil-ities. Stay on top of evolving emotions in the teams as expressed in meetings, reports, or surveys, or in informal exchanges between team members. Ensure that positive, helpfulness, and morale-building are always present in these exchanges.
- **Discourage cliques, gossip about others, or any other manifestation of disunity**. Explicitly discuss relationship stresses or divisions in the team. Strengthen the bonds and the trust between all team members. Team-building activities and team-level social events will also help.
- **Recalibrate negative individual emotions into positive team emotions**. Listen to the concerns and

other negative emotions of individuals as they arise, provide them with your support, and create a relaxed, empathetic culture in which all team members support each other. Train Agile coaches and scrum masters in Emotional Intelligence.

Agile teams are created to deal with change, and change inevitably impacts the emotions of team members and the team as a whole. Although often overlooked, the management of individual and team emotions is one of the most important responsibilities of agile team leaders.

REFERENCES

Affective Leadership in Agile Teams. Max-Antoine Renault, Murat Tarakci. California Management Review (Summer 2023). https://journals.sagepub.com/doi/full/10.1177/00081256231179993

Access this and more *Ideas at* **ideasforleaders.com**

Infectious Generosity

The ultimate idea worth spreading

By Chris Anderson

Penguin/WH Allen; January 2024; 272 pages; ISBN: 978-0-753-560-49-5

Review by Mark McKergow

When Chris Anderson left his computer magazine empire in the early 2000s he can scarcely have known what lay ahead. Taking over the Technology, Entertainment, Design (TED) conference, up to that point an exclusive tech and games event, Anderson made it into a non-profit and wondered how to make a wider audience for TED's lecture-based content. TV executives laughed at him – who would want to watch a lecture? So, he decided to experiment with the new-fangled internet and publish six

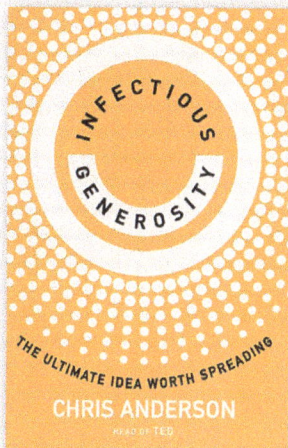

full talks online. Some said he would ruin the business. Others enjoyed the ability to share what they had seen with others, free. And, as we now know, TED has gone from strength-to-strength with vast audiences, communities around the world, TEDx events all over the place – and, yes, a still-thriving live conference arm.

In this book, Chris Anderson starts by reflecting on these events as an early example of infectious generosity; giving that inspires others to give too. Having first given his content and then his brand away, Anderson is well-placed to write about this. He has worked with billionaires and academics, wealthy business leaders and street-smart activists. Nobody gets paid to do a TED talk and so the whole enterprise relies on generosity and the soft power of invitation. TED's tagline is 'ideas worth spreading', and so this book might be seen as the next key step for Anderson and his startling entrepreneur style.

Anderson is clear; giving is not a simple selfless act. Rather, he says, "the decision to be generous can be simultaneously an act of sacrifice and, profoundly, an act in the long-term self-interest of the giver." This kind of giving is not just about supporting good causes, it is about making sure that the ways we give are themselves potential catalysts for other things to happen, more people to get involved, and the process to move from just-sustain-ing to accelerating ahead. And the fact that non-material things can now be distributed at nearly no cost via the web also changes the picture.

The book is in three parts: Why, How and What-If. Why is about how infectious generosity's time has come. Anderson presents a wide-ranging take on how people feel about giving, and to his credit addresses many legitimate points which can make us nervous both of giving and of other givers. Why should crazy billionaires get so much influence? Isn't it the role of governments to sort out (insert your issue here)? Presenting original research carried out by the TED community, Anderson shows how giving has multiple affects on both the recipient and the giver. Both feel good about it, both benefit from it – but the happiness generated by giving is far greater for the recipient than it would have been for the giver spending the money on themselves.

The How section very sensibly starts with non-financial giving. There are so many things we can give and share which make a difference: attention, knowledge, connection, hospitality and enchantment can all make huge differences and don't cost money. Moving on to financial affairs, Anderson is keen to show how the stories that go along with the money may be even more important than the cash; those are what inspire others to join. The What-If section shares provocative ideas

The decision to be generous can be simultaneously an act of sacrifice and, profoundly, an act in the long-term self-interest of the giver.

and examples; I was particularly taken with shipping giant Maersk who, faced with climate change, funded a research hub to investigate zero-carbon shipping and invited their competitors to join them. Greener fuels are now becoming a reality. (This is a wonderful example of 'leading as a host', where the power of invitation creates new possibilities and connections.) Anderson closes with thoughts on 'how much'; Christian tithing (from income) and Islamic zakat (from wealth) guidelines are a starting point.

This book is an original and important contribution, which will be read by business leaders who want to act more broadly about how they use their resources to open new options and break out of zero-sum financial thinking.

Dr Mark McKergow is an author, speaker and consultant based in Edinburgh. He pioneered the Solutions Focus and Host Leadership approaches to building progress in tough situations.

The AI-Savvy Leader

9 ways to take
back control and
make AI work

By David De Cremer

HBR Press; June 2024; 256 pages:
ISBN: 978-1-647-826-23-9

B i g   D a t a,
Machine Learn-
ing now Artifi-
cial Intelligence – the incremental waves of the
new abilities of computing power keep surging forward.
So far, the bang has been slightly less than the hype –
but with each new cycle of this progress, the impact is
slightly greater.

The flip-side of this story is that while AI, and before
it Big Data and Machine Learning, and to a lesser extent
virtual world technologies, will transform our worlds – so
far the change has been peripheral while the investment
has been extravagant. The business world continues
to splurge cash on AI, few companies other than the
chip-makers, Nvidia at the forefront, are reaping the
benefits yet.

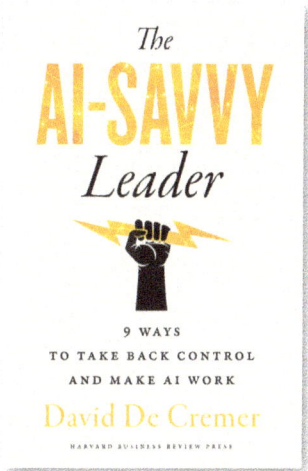

This book from David De Cremer suggests that, much like the earlier waves of digital transformation, successful implementation of AI will only occur when the organizations and the leaders of those organizations are able to weave the benefits of AI across the whole business strategy, rather than as an add-on. He also sees that AI is different to the previous waves – it will affect business much more profoundly, and it will affect everyone.

De Cremer opens this book with the crux of the problem – a story of how an organization invests huge sums in AI to make its processes leaner and more efficient and a year on pull-the-plug, as little efficiency is being realized while the cash continues to race into a blackhole. The reason he posits – and the question he regularly asks of executive boards – 'where were the business leaders in this AI adoption project?'. They never fully got their heads around what this 'new employee – AI' could do, where it would fit in – and when questions needed answering around this issue, they deferred to the techies, and not the business-oriented executives. The leadership were side-lining themselves.

With leadership not being where it needed to be, the essential ingredients for a successful digital transformation project – namely, empowering and motivating people, providing guidance, and

*instilling a work culture where people learn from
their failures – were not delivered.*

The sector reports a staggering rate of failure: $6.8bn
was invested in AI projects in 2023, with an 87% failing
to reach their objectives. As always with technology, the
issue is not the tech part, but the human part. Executives
see that AI is 'a big thing' and they should 'act fast' not
to get left behind, but it is hugely complex and they don't
really understand it – these two forces 'urgency' vs 'slight
knowledge' create a tension, that means they stand back
and let others take the lead.

As with all complex issues, us poor humans need
to distil things down to simple, clear paradigms – and
De Cremer does just this. His work suggests that the AI
world fall into two distinct camps:

- **Perspective 1** – AI is an increasingly cheap way to
  replace people and achieve new levels of productivity
  and efficiency.
- **Perspective 2** – It's a powerful tool to augment – but
  not replace – human intelligence and unlock more
  innovation and creativity in workers.

Perspective 1 is very much where we have been and
many companies still are – it is 19th and 20th century
business thinking, that the bottom line and efficiency is
the only thing that matters. That we can use the logical

deduction of AI to determine how to use AI further. This way chaos lies though. The author believes the AI-Savvy leader must view the world through Perspective 2 – and anyone who has used ChatGPT will probably agree – it can augment creativity, and speed it along, but it still requires human judgement and evaluation to make it work well.

Ultimately, humans still need humans to operate effectively. It is the secret sauce of humanity, the junk code that makes us human, that is needed. And that is what good leaders can leverage.

The book that follows this opening insight is closely focused on how the main and familiar elements of leadership can be applied and directed specifically to AI transformation. The chapter headings are all central elements of good leadership: Learning; Purpose; Communication; Emotional Intelligence and so on.

An elegant example of this is in the chapter on *Empathy: Using a Human-centred Approach to AI Adoption*. De Cremer recounts a story with a CTO who employs an AI algorithm to assess the quality of marketing reports, and by association their authors. The eventual outcome is that the relentless monitoring and assessing, allied to the inevitable variation in quality that employees delivered over a time period, ground them down. Absenteeism and staff turnover increased. De Cremer points out that humans are not designed to be relentlessly consistent; what he terms 'reflective procrastination' is a human habit that occurs frequently, it is creative and allows different perspectives to be viewed. While it upsets the consistency metrics, it can boost morale, insights and creativity. In the long-run it is highly valuable, but in the short-term seems inefficient. The code did not allow for that – but good leaders understand it. With the code suitable tweaked for the human condition things picked-up again. The book is filled with these little insights.

De Cremer covers these human issues that too often derail AI implementation projects: tackling the isolation that AI use can create; the frequency of communicating about AI development to reassure workers and dispel fears of impending unemployment; expressing your vision in human, not technical or efficiency terms – sell the benefits; the imperative of having to stay current in your awareness of AI developments...

The AI-Savvy Leader's objective is to deliver a more efficient organization which uses AI effectively. That will still be an organization run and staffed by humans – and it will be those humans that determine whether the AI is used effectively and productively or not. The AI-Savvy Leader – like all leaders – therefore needs to focus on the human reactions to the new technology and not the other way around.

The Neurodiversity Edge

The essential guide to embracing autism, ADHD, dyslexia and other neurological differences for any organization

By Maureen Dunne

John Wiley & Sons; March 2024; 279 pages; ISBN: 978-1-394-199-28-0

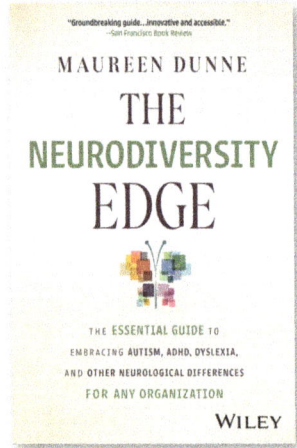

"Groundbreaking guide...innovative and accessible."
—San Francisco Book Review

MAUREEN DUNNE

THE NEURODIVERSITY EDGE

THE ESSENTIAL GUIDE TO EMBRACING AUTISM, ADHD, DYSLEXIA, AND OTHER NEUROLOGICAL DIFFERENCES FOR ANY ORGANIZATION

WILEY

There is an irony that while a significant number of the great technological, scientific and cultural breakthroughs of humanity have been achieved by 'mavericks' - those who do not fit in with the popular construct – organizations continue to seek those who do. Many now think that Thomas Edison suffered from ADHD. Richard Branson famously failed to achieve any public exams, due to his dyslexia, and has subsequently been diagnosed as having ADHD too. However, in a 2020 survey of UK employers, the author notes that "50% openly admitted that they would not hire a neurodivergent job seeker"

How can neurodivergent people be responsible for a disproportionate share of our innovations while most are so strikingly left out of the economy or on the margins of society?

Maureen Dunne, the author of this book, is a cognitive scientist, who asks "how can neurodivergent people be responsible for a disproportionate share of our important innovations while most are so strikingly left out of the economy or on the margins of society?"

Part of the issue is that the spectrum we identify neurodivergency on is so wide that that many people are not confident on how to react to it. Where do we place those with ADHD, dyslexia, dyspraxia, dyscalculia, dysgraphia, misophonia, stammering... we know that having any of these conditions is entirely independent from your intelligence. Some with these conditions will be brilliant, others less so – just like amongst the neurotypical.

Neurodiversity, as Dunne describes, just means those who think in a different way to the majority. The majority being termed 'neurotypical'. The crucial concept being that being neurotypical is neither better nor worse than being neurodivergent for many; it is just probably easier, as being part of the mainstream is usually a less challenging existence than being part of the periphery. The world tends to be shaped for the mainstream and those who do not fit that, have to adapt to work with it.

This book is both a call for organizations to accommodate neurodiversity – as much, if not more, for their own benefit as for the neurodiverse – and a guide on how they can do that.

We live in a world that likes to think in linear terms. Dunne opens the book with a quote from Edwin Abbot's 1884 book Flatland, that tries to describe to people who see the world in two-dimensions, what the third dimension can offer them – and this is the richness that she explains we are missing out on, by only looking at problems, processes and people in a singular way of thinking, that of the neurotypical. How much are we missing by not embracing alternative ways of viewing issues?

The case against groupthink and in favour of different ways of thinking – be they lateral thinking, hyperfocus, visual thinking, dyslexic thinking, pattern thinking, bottom-up thinking, reverse engineering or many others, is easy enough to set-out, and Dunne does so clearly and compellingly.

The challenge is in the 'How do we enable this' part, that makes up two-thirds of the book. And as with just about every organizational challenge, the answer lies not in some clever technical solution or innovation, or even some new framework – but in ages-old human behaviours. It is about culture and mindset.

At the heart of the book lies Dunne's 5-step Pyramid of Neuroinclusion. She describes it as: "*...a layered set of objectives that...must all be cemented into place to bring about lasting authentic neuroinclusion...*"

The five layers are: 'trust and psychological safety'; 'transparent communications'; 'universal design principles at work'; 'auxiliary support accessibility'; 'universal empathy' leading to 'authentic neurodiversity inclusion'.

Dunne weaves these approaches through the remainder of the book. There is an important chapter on 'Recruiting for Diversity' that sets out the strategies needed to be borne in mind to do this well'. And more closely on the layers themselves, one – close to Ideas for Leaders hearts – on 'Accommodating Humans', which recognizes that everyone is different, and that what fits many doesn't fit all. This is part of Universal Design, and its Seven Principles. And another on 'Workplace Flexibility' which deals with auxiliary support flexibility. And the last of the section on universal empathy.

Dunne's conclusion on why neurodiversity is so important today, is well worth reflecting on. We live in 'the transformation age' where change occurs at increasing velocity, and it is far harder to describe what the world will look like a decade ahead, than it has ever been before.

This is principally driven by technological advances, with today's focus on AI and AGI.

AGI, as we currently can predict it, still works on a linear basis of data curation. In order for us to come up with the truly revolutionary new ideas, rather than the incrementally improved ones, we will still need out-of-the-box thinking, and that tends to come from non-linear thought. As Dunne puts it an AI trained on baroque music of Bach, Handel and Corelli could generate new pieces, but they would be largely indistinguishable from the pieces they learnt from – there would be no Moonlight Sonata. If we are to create future Moonlight Sonatas in a wide range of subject areas, we will need greater cognitive diversity. As she says, embracing "authentic neurodiversity as a core organizational value... is not the whole solution to anything, but it is part of the solution to nearly everything."

Organizations need to structure themselves in such a way that they can leverage this talent. In such a way that they are embracing cognitive diversity and making those who can bring it to their organizations be transparently valued and comfortable to be doing so.

Adapted from the review in **www.IdeasforLeaders.com/book-reviews/**

About the Publishers

Ideas for Leaders

Ideas for Leaders summarizes the thinking of
the foremost researchers and experts on leadership and management
practice from the world's top business schools and management
research institutions. With these concise and easily readable 'Ideas'
you can quickly and easily inform yourself and your colleagues about
the latest insights into management best practice.

The research-based Ideas are supported by a growing series of
podcasts with influential thinkers, CEOs, and other leading leadership
and management experts from large organizations and small. We also
publish book reviews and a new series of online programs.

www.ideasforleaders.com

The Center for the Future of Organization (CFFO)

CFFO is an independent Think Tank and Research Center at the
Drucker School of Management at Claremont Graduate University.
The Center's mission is to deepen our understanding of new
capabilities that are critical to succeed in a digitally connected world,
and to support leaders and organizations along their transformational
journey.

In the tradition of Peter Drucker, the Center works across disciplines,
combining conceptual depth with practical applicability and ethical
responsibility, in close collaboration and connection with thought
leaders and practice leaders from academia, business, and consulting.

www.futureorg.org

DLQ Advisory Board

Developing**Leaders**
Quarterly

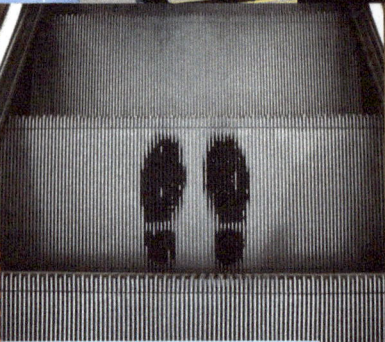